BRITAIN'S BEST POLITICAL CARTOONS 2

Dr Tim Benson is Britain's leading authority on political cartoons. He runs the Political Cartoon Gallery & Café, which is located near the River Thames in Putney. He has produced numerous books on the history of cartoons, including *David Low Censored*, *Giles's War: Cartoons 1939–45*, *Churchill in Caricature*, *Low and the Dictators*, *The Cartoon Century: Modern Britain through the Eyes of Its Cartoonists*, *Drawing the Curtain: The Cold War in Cartoons*, *Over the Top: A Cartoon History of Australia at War*, *Britain's Best Ever Political Cartoons* and *How to be British: A Cartoon Celebration*.

BRITAIN'S BEST POLITICAL CARTOONS 2022

Edited by Tim Benson

HUTCHINSON

HEINEMANN

In memory of Anthony Mourek, a great cartoon connoisseur

1 3 5 7 9 10 8 6 4 2

Hutchinson Heinemann
20 Vauxhall Bridge Road London SW1V 2SA

Hutchinson Heinemann is part of the
Penguin Random House group of companies whose addresses
can be found at global.penguinrandomhouse.com.

Penguin
Random House
UK

First published in the United Kingdom by Hutchinson Heinemann in 2022.

A CIP catalogue record for this book is available from the British Library.

ISBN 9781529153057

Typeset in 11/15.5 pt Amasis MT Light by Jouve (UK), Milton Keynes

Printed and bound in Italy by L.E.G.O. S.p.A.

The authorised representative in the EEA is Penguin Random House
Ireland, Morrison Chambers, 32 Nassau Street, Dublin D02 YH68

Penguin Random House is committed to a sustainable future
for our business, our readers and our planet. This book is made
from Forest Stewardship Council® certified paper.

FSC
www.fsc.org

MIX
Paper from
responsible sources
FSC® C018179

INTRODUCTION

In their infinite wisdom, the publishers of this anthology have decided to pay Prince Harry a princely sum to write his royal memoir. I believed – wrongly, as it turned out – that if I focused on the monarchy this year, I might be similarly remunerated . . . Anyway, as it is the year of the Queen's Platinum Jubilee, I deemed it as good a time as any to examine how Britain's finest political cartoonists have portrayed the Royal Family over the past few centuries. I am not the first to write on this subject. My focus, however, is rather different from those – such as Michael Wynn-Jones and Kenneth Baker – who have gone before. They considered how cartoons illustrate particular historical events. My intention in this essay is to put the cartoons front and centre, showing how and why the portrayal of royal subjects has changed, and what impact this has had on both cartoonists and the royalty they set out to caricature.

It has to be admitted that, from the very beginning, the relationship between cartoonists and their royal subjects has tended to be a tense one.

'Take them away! I do not understand these madde designes!' the famously petulant and vain Charles I said when confronted with an early example of a less-than-respectful engraving. 'I don't understand these caricatures!' muttered George III the following century when shown prints by the father of the modern political cartoon, James Gillray. George III's bewilderment was understandable. Gillray targeted the king with a disrespect and a viciousness that had not been seen before, savaging him during his periodic bouts of madness, while at other times depicting him as both a pretentious buffoon and a miser. *Temperance Enjoying a Frugal Meal* (published in 1792) is typical of Gillray's output. It shows the king surrounded by the trappings of royalty, yet dining on a meagre meal of eggs and sauerkraut and utilising the tablecloth as a napkin. For its part, *A Connoisseur Examining a Cooper*, published the same year, is Gillray's response to George III's disparaging view of the cartoonist's work. It depicts the king squinting at a miniature of Oliver Cromwell, the infamous overthrower of the Stuart monarchy, going out of its way to contrast this almost regal portrayal of Cromwell (who famously told the portraitist Samuel Cooper to show him with 'warts and all') with a gawping George III. Given the outbreak of the French Revolution just three years before and the recent assassination of King Gustav III of Sweden, the republican undertones of the cartoon are all too clear.

Gillray's *A Connoisseur Examining a Cooper* (1792).

Less than a decade later, however, Gillray radically changed tack. With the start of the Napoleonic wars and – at one point – the seemingly very real prospect of an invasion by the French, patriotism, not mockery, became the order of the day. The enemy now was Bonaparte – or 'Little Boney', as Gillray described him – and his evil band of revolutionaries. The hero was the previously derided king, who now became 'Farmer George' (a nickname derived from George III's interest in rural affairs), a symbol of all that was good about England. A cartoon from 1803 set the new tone. It shows George III inspecting a tiny Napoleon and saying, in an echo of the King of Brobdingnag in Swift's *Gulliver's Travels*, 'I cannot but consider you to be one of the most pernicious little odious reptiles that nature ever suffer'd to crawl upon the surface of the Earth . . .' Not surprisingly, George III was reported to be much happier with Gillray's new approach.

Not that the cartoonist had undergone a total conversion. He might now have been prepared to treat George III respectfully, but he was unsparing in his treatment of the king's son, the Prince of Wales (later Prince Regent and, in time, King George IV), savaging his friends and mistresses, gleefully recording his reputation for excess and debauchery and, in so doing, creating a visual image of the prince that persists to this day.

A Voluptuary Under the Horrors of Digestion shows an overweight and decadent prince bursting out of his waistcoat. *L'Assemblée Nationale*, in its depiction of the Whig leader Charles James Fox, his friends and (cut off deliberately by the right-hand margin) George himself, ruthlessly mocks the prince's political circle of friends. So outraged was the Prince of Wales when *L'Assemblée Nationale* appeared in 1804 that he offered a large sum of money to have both the prints and the original copperplate destroyed. He was unsuccessful on both fronts.

Paradoxically, while he hated how Gillray portrayed him, the prince was an avid collector of the cartoonist's work. In July 1803, he opened an account at a shop in St James's owned by Hannah Humphrey, a leading London print seller whom Gillray had worked for exclusively since 1791. The Prince of Wales's purchases included an 1807 series of satirical drawings by Gillray portraying Lady Emma Hamilton, the noted beauty, as an ungainly frump – drawings which are still in the royal collection today.

When Gillray died in June 1815, the cartoonist George Cruikshank assumed his mantel. But he proved to be more easily bought than his predecessor had been. A spate of mocking cartoons gave way to a series of rather more flattering ones after the receipt of a £100 royal bribe. When the Prince Regent came to the throne as George IV in 1820, Cruikshank was again financially induced 'not to caricature His Majesty in any immoral situation'.

George IV's niece, Victoria, who assumed the throne in 1837, experienced both mockingly satirical and cloyingly deferential treatment at the hands of the cartoonists who recorded her long reign. *Punch* magazine, which began its illustrious 150-year run in 1841, began with the former approach (particularly in its depiction of the queen's consort, Prince Albert). But over time – as it became increasingly more establishment-minded – it adopted the latter stance, to the point where, after Albert's untimely death, it was accused of producing 'sycophantic drivel' by one unimpressed commentator. For its part, *Punch*'s first imitator, *Judy*, maintained a certain reverence for the monarchy.

The more radical *Fun* and *Tomahawk* magazines, by contrast, were critical of the queen, particularly when, after Albert's death, she withdrew from public life. *Tomahawk*'s lead cartoonist and joint editor, Matthew Morgan, proved to be a particularly persistent royal gadfly. His depiction of an empty throne entitled *Where is Britannia?*, which was published in June 1867, nearly six years after Albert's demise, caused a storm. So too did *A Brown Study!*, published just two months later, which strongly insinuated that John Brown, Victoria's devoted manservant, was exerting an unhealthy hold over her (*Tomahawk* experienced public opprobrium over its decision to publish the cartoon but also saw its circulation increase to 50,000 – close to that of *Punch*). In the summer of 1867, Morgan also took aim at the Prince of Wales (later Edward VII) in *I'll Follow Thee!*, which depicted the prince as Hamlet, straining to follow the ghost of George IV into a life of debauchery. Morgan sought to conceal his identity by signing his cartoons with a small tomahawk rather than his name. But he was unable to preserve his anonymity for long. It was said at the time that, such was the backlash against the publication of *I'll Follow Thee!*, that Morgan was forced to flee the country (the more prosaic explanation for his departure is that he needed to escape his creditors).

Popular wisdom has it that Queen Victoria embodied the strait-laced stuffiness that defined her reign and that she was humourless. Her response to a jest – 'We are not amused' – has become legendary (and probably is). The fact remains, though, that she amassed around 8,000 Georgian cartoons in the course of her reign ('She scooped up whole collections,' according to Kate Heard, a curator at the Royal Collection Trust). Among them were many by Thomas Rowlandson, who set out to satirise the absurd fashions of his era and revelled

Matthew Morgan's controversial cartoon *A Brown Study!* (1867) shows Queen Victoria's manservant, John Brown, casually leaning over the vacant throne and toying with the British lion.

in aristocratic and political scandals. (One cartoon in the royal collection, for example, ridicules the Duchess of Devonshire, who gained a reputation for kissing voters to secure their support for Charles James Fox in the 1784 election, by depicting her in a passionate embrace with a butcher.) The queen even bought the collection of the publisher Samuel Fores, whom her uncle had considered suing in 1788 for his unflattering cartoons of the then Prince of Wales's unsuccessful attempts to be made regent during one of his father's bouts of illness. Her Majesty, it would seem, could take a joke.

Occasional sniping at royalty remained a constant during the reign of Victoria's successors, Edward VII and George V, and persisted even amid the torrent of patriotism that accompanied the First World War. The *Daily Herald* and its cartoonist Will Dyson, for example, couldn't look past the German ancestry of George V and were happy to ridicule it. The king was certainly not amused. According to the *Star*, he became 'so angry' about Dyson's cartoons that the censors 'received orders to "put the soft pedal" on all war cartoons in the magazines and newspapers'. The War Office was even put under pressure by Buckingham Palace to make a ruling that such cartoons could not be sent to soldiers serving at the front. The *Star* criticised the king's actions as 'entirely selfish' and 'absolutely at odds with English public opinion'. *Punch*, meanwhile, continued the unashamed grovelling

towards the Royal Family that had been its policy since the reign of Queen Victoria, publishing cartoon after cartoon of Mr Punch bowing and scraping in front of whoever the monarch of the day happened to be. Maybe this was one reason why so many *Punch* cartoonists received knighthoods.

"I know, Sir, that you will maintain the prestige of the Title. It would be impossible to increase it."

A *Punch* cartoon commemorates the investiture of the Prince of Wales (later King George V) in November 1901. Mr Punch, seen bowing before the prince, illustrates the publication's absolute deference to the monarchy.

Soon, as peace returned to Europe, other publications started to follow *Punch*'s lead. Deference became most apparent among the daily newspapers (for whom the inclusion of cartoons was a relatively recent development). They were, after all, run by press barons who were either peers or aspired to join the peerage. A convention even became established that royal faces should not be shown in cartoons. Looking back on the interwar period, Leslie Illingworth, a former cartoonist for the *Daily Mail*, recalled:

> You seemed to put your top hat on when you drew Royal cartoons. I did very few of them and wished I could have avoided it. It was like drawing a religious cartoon and I didn't do those very well either. It was not like today when people can be very rude. I am an old, old man, and in those days your editor expected solemn treatment of Royalty.

The Australian-born cartoonist David Low, who had often featured George V as a figure of fun when he'd worked for the *Sydney Bulletin*, discovered after his arrival in England in 1919 that no such licence was permitted in the mother country. 'I cannot regard it as a triumph of loyalty, but only of sycophancy, that no periodical in England will publish my caricature of the reigning monarch,' he said. 'When a few years ago I published a faithful caricature of the Prince of Wales there were the usual squeaks of "Bolshevik".'

Those cartoonists who did dare criticise the monarchy (and those publications prepared to include their work) were few and far between. One of this rare group was Desmond Rowney, who drew under the pen name Maro. Public-school-educated and a former British army officer (he was court-marshalled in 1921), he was a staunch communist, who became notorious for his unflattering portrayals of King George V in the *Daily Worker*. During the king's Silver Jubilee, Rowney drew a number of cartoons excoriating what he regarded as the profligacy of the celebrations at a time of national recession and high unemployment. His anti-monarchy stance drew police attention. A year before the Jubilee he ran foul of Princess Marina of Greece and Denmark for his less-than-flattering cartoon of her marriage to George V's son, Prince George. She indignantly reproduced the offending cartoon in the newsletter of her organisation, the Christian Protest Movement. Rowney responded by informing her that his copyright had been infringed and demanding a reproduction fee of two pounds and two shillings. He was sent a guinea. Unsurprisingly, Rowney

POTTERY WORKERS ARE REPORTED TO BE WORKING OVERTIME ON "JUBILEE MUGS". "MARO" OFFERS HIS SUGGESTION.

Rowney's cartoon for the *Daily Worker*, published on 8 February 1935, mocks the lavish celebrations for the king's Silver Jubilee. The motto of the royal family, 'Dieu et mon droit' ('God and my right'), is replaced with 'Dieu et mon dough'.

proved to be the only cartoonist to cover the death of King George V in January 1936. Other publications deemed the occasion too solemn to be marred by the frivolity of a cartoon.

If there was one moment between the wars when the overwhelmingly monarchist sentiment of the national press was put under pressure, it was the abdication crisis that followed hot on the heels of the accession of the new monarch, Edward VIII. But, to a man, newspaper proprietors agreed to keep the king's romance with the twice-married American divorcée Wallis Simpson secret. The *Daily Express* even went so far as to remove Mrs Simpson from a photograph taken of her with the king onboard the royal yacht. Those British readers who bought American newspapers and magazines from local shops rather than by post found that some passages had been mysteriously cut out with scissors. As the crisis reached its peak, Lord Beaverbrook, proprietor of the *Evening Standard* 'issued instructions that no cartoons on personalities involved should be published'.

The *Standard*'s cartoonist, David Low, decided to put Beaverbrook's resolve to the test. He drew a cartoon featuring three portraits hanging on a wall, two of which were of Wallis Simpson's previous husbands, Mr Spencer and Mr Simpson, and the third of which was of Edward VIII. He called it *The Wallis Collection*. The cartoon was not published, and the original drawing was later destroyed. 'Low,' concluded *Cavalcade* magazine, 'is allowed to take his own line in politics, often goes against the *Standard*'s Conservative policy, but there are limits,

The Wallis Collection, originally by David Low, was destroyed before it could be published, but is here reimagined by Steve Bright.

Difficult Days for Low (published on 9 December 1936) mocks Lord Beaverbrook's censorship of any cartoons relating to the abdication crisis.

and some of his cartoons – one of them on the abdication – were killed.' Annoyed, he drew *Difficult Days for Low*, showing himself locked in a steam room and being told by Beaverbrook that he would not be allowed out until he promised not to do another cartoon on the crisis. Unlike *The Wallis Collection*, *Difficult Days* was published.

Media deference towards the Royal Family not only survived Edward VIII's successor, George VI, and the turmoil of the Second World War, but lasted well into the reign of Elizabeth II. In doing so, however, it did no more than match the public mood. The Queen's accession at the age of just 27, following her father's early death, was accompanied by a national wave of patriotic fervour. As former *Daily Express* cartoonist Osbert Lancaster put it: 'Everyone loved Queen Elizabeth so much and felt so sorry for George VI having to take the throne against his wishes that any real criticism was unthinkable after the dignified heroism and dedication during the war years.'

David Low struck a rare note of criticism amid the general euphoria. Feeling, like Rowney before him, that the cost of the royal jamboree was hard to justify at a time of economic austerity, he produced a cartoon for the *Guardian* entitled *Morning After*, which shows middle-aged adults in nappies crawling amid bunting, champagne and books of fairy princess stories across a floor on which the words '£100,000,000 spree' appear and on which a television set stands, displaying the face of 'reality'. The message did not go down well. 'Scandalous and vulgar,' wrote one of Low's many critics; 'the humour of a very small minority who only harbour envy, hatred and malice in their hearts'. 'What execrable bad taste!' said another. As sackfuls of hate mail appeared, the *Guardian*'s editor, A. P. Wadsworth, felt he had no option but to apologise formally for allowing the cartoon to appear. Support for Low was in short supply, although Malcolm Muggeridge, who became *Punch* editor in the same year as the coronation, agreed with the cartoonist that things had gone too far, and argued that the monarchy had become 'a sort of substitute religion' and 'a focus for sycophancy'. He was sufficiently alert to the public mood, however, not to allow criticism of the monarchy in the pages of his magazine. He simply ignored its existence.

It was not until the 1960s that what some felt to be a long-overdue change in public attitudes to the Royal Family started to take root. Deference declined. More criticism was voiced. Even so, most cartoonists continued to toe a royalist line. Carl Giles, a former cartoonist for the *Daily Express*, considered himself a 'leftie' but was nevertheless a staunch supporter of the Royal Family:

> I make a distinction between pulling their legs and taking the mickey. The first is fun, the second is snide. I don't begrudge the Queen any of my taxes for trooping the colour. We would get greyer and greyer without the Royal Family. Thank God for 'em.

Giles's colleague on the *Daily Express*, Michael Cummings, echoed his sentiments: 'When just about every other institution in this country is working badly, Royalty remains one of the things you can still truly admire.'

Many other cartoonists were similarly reluctant to mock the sovereign, not least because it was considered ungentlemanly to ridicule a woman, especially a queen, in a manner that caricature typically demands. Stanley Franklin recalled that in his first few years as a cartoonist on the *Mirror* he was allowed to draw only the back view of the Queen for that reason. Cummings considered himself one of the Queen's most loyal subjects, and so he felt inhibited when it came to depicting her: 'When you meet her she really is a good-looking woman, fine eyes and complexion, charming smile. But photographs of her don't do her justice and caricatures, emphasising recognisable features of her like her teeth, can make her look ugly.' He also felt uncomfortable drawing the young Prince Charles because the cartoonist in him inevitably wanted to exaggerate the size of his ears: 'One reader wrote and said how beastly I was to make his ears so big, because now he'd be ragged unmercifully at school. I felt rather guilty.' When John Jensen innocently drew the Queen as a middle-aged woman, the *Sunday Telegraph* was inundated with complaints. 'Her majesty was represented as an unattractive frumpish woman, which she certainly is not,' wrote one reader. Others argued that the cartoon was

'My more spirited subjects used to globetrot while *I* stayed at home. What are all *your* Sir Walter Raleighs doing?'

John Jensen's cartoon of an 'unattractive frumpish woman' for the *Sunday Telegraph* (20 February 1977).

'tactless' and 'unnecessary'. 'All I did,' Jensen protested, 'was to try and draw the Queen accurately as a middle-aged woman'. As he later told me, this did not stop Prince Philip, an avid cartoon collector, from buying the original.

It was not until the 1980s that the days of cartooning reticence showed signs, if not of drawing to a close exactly, at least of being in decline. Arguably Prince Charles had tempted fate in 1978 when he questioned how the courtesy that the Royal Family were so used to receiving could have survived into the modern age: 'I cannot help but reflect on how politely we have been treated,' he said, 'compared to the way King George III and his family were treated by the 18th and 19th century cartoonists.' Even so, few, if any, cartoonists were ever prepared to go to the extremes to be witnessed on the decade's most popular satirical programme, *Spitting Image*, first aired in 1984. Here, the Royal Family were grotesquely and often savagely portrayed as a bunch of rubbery puppet misfits. Princess Margaret was shown as permanently tipsy, Princess Anne appeared as grumpy, the Queen Mother was depicted as a gin-swigging granny, and Prince Andrew was labelled 'Randy Andy'. Royal sketches were removed from the first episode before it was broadcast out of courtesy to Prince Philip, who was due to open the East Midlands Television Centre, but they were later reinstated.

Princess Diana was to reveal that the Royal Family 'hated' the show. She, however, professed that she 'absolutely adored it'.

Nick Garland's cartoon for the *Daily Telegraph* (16 November 1976) illustrates how the tone of royal cartoons was beginning to shift in the 1970s. Total deference now made way for occasional interrogation and mockery.

I asked some of today's cartoonists what they thought of the modern monarchy. 'Oh Christ! Don't get me started on those parasites!' was the immediate response of Dave Brown, cartoonist for the *Independent* (prompting me to think as I transcribed his view, 'Well there goes any chance of a knighthood.') His unflattering view is not unique. Steve Bell, political cartoonist for the *Guardian*, thinks the Royal Family are a 'gross anachronism and a terrible sign of a lack of maturity of our democratic process'. 'Why', asks Bell, 'should this upper-class person, there simply due to act of birth, be there? Why should we swear fealty to her? It strikes me as nonsensical.' Tim Sanders, pocket cartoonist for the *Independent*, concurs with Bell's view: he doesn't believe 'in hereditary power and wealth'. Patrick Blower, cartoonist for the *Daily Telegraph*, is convinced the institution is an 'obsolete soap opera. If one were creating a nation from scratch now, no sane person would start with a hereditary monarchy.'

When push comes to shove, however, few of the cartoonists I spoke to actually want to see the back of the monarchy. Steven Camley of the *Herald Scotland* prefers to view himself as a 'soft monarchist' who 'can see and appreciate the benefits and prestige the monarchy brings to "Global Britain", but I wouldn't call myself a dyed-in-the-wool monarchist in the sense I have all the commemorative tea towels.' Andy Davey, political cartoonist for the *Daily Telegraph*, muses that the alternative to hereditary monarchy – an elected president model – would be worse:

As I think of who on earth we might actually elect as a President, I shudder – President

Farage? President Clarkson? President F*cking Johnson!? . . . I guess the major problem is the baggage, the extended family and the associated remnants of the aristocracy that prevent overhaul of the crusty bits of our society.

There's a degree of self interest in all this. According to both Nicola Jennings of the *Guardian* and Kathryn Lamb, pocket cartoonist for *Private Eye* and the *Spectator*, the Royal Family are too useful as cartooning fodder for them to be dispensed with. 'My heart says republican,' Lamb confesses, 'but my head says royalist just because getting rid of them would deprive cartoonists of a ready target and source of humour! . . . The tradition of royal awfulness goes back a long way through the centuries and is fascinating,' she adds. 'William and Kate are quite extraordinarily bland [by comparison], but still caricaturable.' Jennings is of the opinion that

It would be a shame not to have the monarchy to poke fun at. It also creates a context from which to satirise British society as a whole – which values them so highly – for the pomposity, sense of superiority, and sycophancy which are as much responsible for creating the illusion of monarchy as are the Royal Family members themselves. Also, they are good clothes horses, and their costumes make a change from the ubiquitous grey suit.

In comparison to many in the public eye – notably politicians – the Royal Family tend to come off quite lightly at the hands of the cartoonists. Peter Schrank, whose work appears in the *Economist*, *Guardian* and *The Times*, says that he is prepared to pull his punches because they 'didn't exactly volunteer for their role' and the Queen is now 'elderly and frail'. Others – notably Steven Camley – argue that because the royals don't have that much impact on our daily lives they don't merit the same volume of criticism and vitriol that is directed at others. It's interesting to note in this regard that, during the long Platinum Jubilee weekend, most cartoons that referenced the celebrations did so purely to attack the Prime Minister, who some felt was using the Jubilee to distract from his own troubles (just two of the cartoons published in national papers paid explicit tribute to the Queen's unprecedented 70-year reign).

The political leanings of newspapers and their readers serve as further buttresses to this tendency towards overall restraint. As Andy Davey says of his own paper:

Peter Schrank used his Jubilee cartoon for *The Times* (3 July 2022) to mock the prime minister, who the day before had commented that he was 'very, very surprised' to receive a fine for attending a birthday party during lockdown. Sue Gray's report into partygate had revealed a drunken party culture within Number 10.

In the *Telegraph*, I imagine the readership would have heart attacks en masse if I were [allowed to be] disrespectful to Her Maj. I like to preserve my disgust for our respected Prime Minister and to depict the Queen as anything other than a saint these days would be foolish and out-of-whack with popular opinion.

Paul Thomas concurs that it is sometimes necessary to paint the monarchy and the government with a different brush: 'There is an awareness that the readers of the *Mail/Express* are likely to be royalists and therefore more likely to be offended by cruel portrayals . . . Having said that,' he adds, 'I've always been very careful to give Charles preposterous ears and to give Camilla a dangerously long chin.'

Inevitably, though, not all subscribe to soft-pedalling treatment of the royals. Nicola Jennings is of the opinion that 'everyone in public life should be a subject of satire.' Nick Newman, pocket cartoonist for the *Sunday Times* and *Spectator*, among others, agrees that 'everyone in authority should be held to account. Respect has to be earned, not given unconditionally.' Wally Fawkes (aka Trog), former cartoonist for the *Observer* and *Punch*, puts it more bluntly: 'Royalty should be treated as people and not as related to God. It would have been very insulting to make Charles's ears small.' For his part, Tim Sanders treats 'the rich and powerful with a uniform level of contempt and ridicule (not that they're bothered or even notice!), but within those parameters there are better and worse, so the Queen gets slightly better treatment than her currently newsworthy son.' Some, like Newman, argue that the public as a whole are much more relaxed about criticism of the Royal Family than they once were: '*Spitting Image* helped push down the barriers,' he suggests. Sanders concurs, arguing that the royals (or, as Steve Bright, political cartoonist for the *Sun*, describes them, 'Britain's most dysfunctional family'), 'have lost a lot of their impunity and are lampooned today pretty ferociously'. The younger royals, in particular, often seem to be regarded as fair game: 'Back in the day, it was more light-hearted jokes about Charles talking to plants and Philip's (intended) faux pas,' he says. Now the likes of Prince Andrew, Prince Harry and Meghan Markle can expect quite savage treatment on occasion.

The one time that publications across the political spectrum tend to open up their cartooning firepower on the Royal Family is when, as Patrick Blower puts it, they 'stray off the red carpet of pomp and ceremony and into the political arena'. At that point, he says, they become 'fair game'. Bright is certainly of this view:

> Although they may aim for party political neutrality on all matters, that is a very different thing from being apolitical. Those who wish to do so never seem to find great difficulty in making their views known. So, of course they are entirely legitimate targets for cartoonists, and regular providers of great material.

David Simonds, a freelance cartoonist for the *Evening Standard* and the *Observer*, similarly believes that when the fairy-tale perception of the Royal Family bumps into social and political reality it becomes necessary to take notice: 'When Prince Harry was due to marry Meghan Markle [at Windsor Castle], Windsor Council swept up its homeless population out of public view and that became the topic of the *Observer* cartoon I drew for that weekend.'

Whatever the views of individual cartoonists, there's little doubt that newspaper editors tend to remain highly cautious when it comes to the royals. Patrick Blower was told that both the Prince Andrew and Harry and Meghan sagas were something of a 'no-go area' for him at the *Telegraph*. It was suggested to Paul Thomas at the *Daily Mail* that he needed to give Prince William more hair. The *Guardian* cropped a Steve Bell cartoon which dared to show the Queen's naked bottom. Peter Schrank encountered full-throated editorial opposition when he drew a cartoon of the Queen for the *Mail on Sunday* in 2016:

> I was asked to make a lot of changes. As it went back and forth with the editor, he kept asking me to tone down my caricature of the Queen. In the end she looked about twenty years younger. I had hoped this might lead to more work, but I never heard from them again.

The inevitable consequence of such editorial sensitivities is that some cartoonists self-edit to avoid problems. Steven Camley learned the hard way:

> I did get spoken to after a cartoon on the passing of Princess Margaret, when I did a split panel cartoon contrasting the reaction to that of Diana's (loads of flowers outside the palace with cards saying 'Why?', to half a dozen bunches with cards saying 'Who?'). It didn't go down well with a number of readers. Lesson learned.

As to which member of the Royal Family cartoonists most enjoy drawing, the popular choice would appear to be the late Prince Philip. According to Steve Bell, 'he looked and sounded magnificently bone-headed.' But when it comes to which current royal is the most popular target, the answer is invariably Prince Andrew. 'Prince Andrew has been good to me of late,' says Nick Newman. 'I've drawn a few front-page gags about him for the *Sunday Times* that have proved very popular, and he is easy to draw.' Paul Thomas loves 'drawing fountains of sweat and a signature slice of pizza in his top pocket instead of a handkerchief' – references to Prince Andrew's infamous interview with the BBC's Emily Maitlis, when he countered Virginia Giuffre's claim that he sweated a lot with an insistence that he was incapable of sweating, and said that when he was alleged to have been at a nightclub with her he had actually been at a Pizza Express in Woking with his daughter Princess Beatrice. As a rule, the Queen tends not to come off too badly at the

"Embarrassing the Royal Family - it's what he would have wanted."

Nick Newman's cartoon for the *Sunday Times* (3 April 2022) supports the notion that Prince Andrew may have taken over from his father as political cartoonists' favourite target.

hands of cartoonists. Nicola Jennings, though, enjoys caricaturing her because 'she is such a funny shape and always looks bad tempered; she never smiles,' while Brian Adcock, former cartoonist for the *Independent*, disdainfully extols 'her gormless rubber face beauty . . . She is an example of when inbreeding goes wrong,' he says.

If part of a cartoonist's job is to mock or tease the Royal Family, do they compromise themselves if they then accept a royal honour? It's a conundrum with a long history. Back in the 1930s, David Low was critical of *Punch*'s Bernard Partridge for accepting a knighthood. 'His knighthood troubled me,' Low said, 'for I could not think that critics or commentators ostensibly of satirical temper on public affairs should accept, like other men, the insignia of trammelling loyalties.' Low himself turned down the offer of a knighthood from Ramsay MacDonald's government, though he did accept one many years later in 1962 (his daughter told me he did this more for his wife than for himself as he knew he was dying from emphysema and wanted to ensure that she could use the title 'Lady Low').

More recently, Steve Bell rejected an MBE shortly after Tony Blair became prime minister. 'I thought about it for a nanosecond and then politely declined,' he says. 'It was on the principle that you shouldn't accept honours from the government you are supposed to be mercilessly ripping the shit out of (metaphorically speaking).' By contrast, Peter Brookes, cartoonist for *The Times*, felt it was entirely possible to accept a CBE in 2017 and continue criticising the good and the great just as he always had:

> I am glad to live in a country that recognises cartoonists in this particular way. There will be those who wonder whether Theresa May and others can justifiably say, 'we have got him now.' My feeling is very much that they haven't. I am not going to stop hitting hard. If I was supporting any one party in my cartoons, it would have been a different matter as to whether I accepted or not, but I criticise and satirise all of them, which makes my decision non-political really.

Perhaps the sting in the tail here lies in Brookes' opening observation: 'I am glad to live in a country that recognises cartoonists.' The fact of the matter is that cartoonists have generally received little official praise or recognition for their work. The last to receive a knighthood was Osbert Lancaster, nearly 50 years ago (and it's only fair to point out that he was probably honoured as much for being an architectural historian, stage designer and

Carl Giles arriving at Buckingham Palace to receive his OBE in 1959.

author as for his accomplishments as a cartoonist). Ronald Searle, one of Britain's greatest practitioners, may have received France's prestigious Légion d'Honneur, but in his home country he was passed over for a knighthood. Carl Giles, Britain's most popular cartoonist for the best part of half a century, was only ever awarded an OBE – an honour that the film director Michael Winner once snobbishly described as 'what you get if you clean the toilets well at King's Cross station.' Over two centuries earlier, William Hogarth failed to receive the patronage of either

George I or George II (at one point he was promised a prestigious commission to paint the Royal Family, only to be snubbed at the last moment). Hogarth's response was to do the only thing a cartoonist can do in such circumstances: to lampoon them.

Meanwhile, in this year of the Platinum Jubilee, the cartooning pendulum continues to swing away from 20th-century deference to something more akin to 18th-century mockery, if without the savagery to be found in Gillray's cartoons. Will a countervailing swing set in at some point? Patrick Blower, for one, thinks not. Soon, he says, 'the only class of people it will be safe to lampoon will be white, public-school-educated elites. In that sense, the royals walk around with big targets on their backs.'

Steve Bell created this design for a 'Platinum Liz' mug to mark the Queen's 70 years on the throne. Like Rowney before him, Bell takes aim at the excess of the Jubilee celebrations and shows a rather critical view of Her Majesty.

On the other hand, David Simonds, in his cartoon for the *Evening Standard*, opts for a more celebratory tone on the occasion of the Platinum Jubilee (1 June 2022).

THE CARTOONS

An Ipsos poll showed that Labour leader Sir Keir Starmer had slipped further behind Boris Johnson in the popularity ratings and was now less popular than Ed Miliband, Tony Blair and Neil Kinnock at the same point in their leaderships. Jeremy Corbyn was the only Labour leader to be less popular at the same stage. According to the cartoonist, 'After 40 years ABBA had announced they were getting back together, releasing a new album and putting on a series of concerts. At the same time there was an awful lot of criticism of Starmer, so the idea of former Labour leaders coming together made a pretty gruesome group.'

4 September 2021
Peter Brookes
The Times

Michael Fawcett, the boss of Prince Charles's charity The Prince's Foundation, was facing a possible police investigation over claims that a Saudi Arabian businessman was offered a knighthood and British passport in return for donations to the charity. Dr Mahfouz Marei Mubarak bin Mahfouz donated £1.5 million to the charity, and then received an honorary CBE from Prince Charles in 2016 for 'services to charities in the UK'. Fawcett, who was also a former assistant valet to the Prince of Wales, resigned from his position.

6 September 2021
Morten Morland
The Times

7 September 2021
Patrick Blower
Daily Telegraph

Boris Johnson broke a manifesto commitment when he confirmed that his government would increase taxes to finance the NHS's post-Covid recovery and overhaul social care. The £12 billion per year increase involved a 1.25 percentage point hike in national insurance contributions. Johnson said that the plan would ensure that 'people get the care that they need, in the right place and at the right time' and alleviate 'catastrophic' care costs, but Labour leader Keir Starmer protested that the rise would 'hit working people hard'.

Home Secretary Priti Patel embarked on plans to turn around migrant boats attempting to cross the Channel and send them back to France. According to reports, UK Border Force officials were already starting to train in 'pushback tactics'. It came after witnesses said a record-breaking 1,000 people attempted to cross the Channel on 6 September. French interior minister, Gérald Darmanin, responded that 'safeguarding human lives at sea took priority over considerations of nationality, status and migratory policy.' Meanwhile, the theatre adaption of *Frozen* finally opened in the West End after several postponements due to the pandemic.

9 September 2021
Christian Adams
Evening Standard

An official in the new Taliban regime stated that Afghanistan's women would no longer be permitted to participate in sport. The deputy head of the Taliban's cultural commission, Ahmadullah Wasiq, said it was not necessary or appropriate for women to play sports as it may expose their bodies. According to the cartoonist, '[This was] one of those where I was lucky with the timing. On the Friday night Emma Raducanu had won her semi-final at the US Open, while at exactly the same time in Afghanistan, the Taliban had declared that women would be banned from playing sport.'

11 September 2021
Peter Brookes
The Times

Amazon founder Jeff Bezos was reported to have backed a new 'rejuvenation company' – Altos Labs – that aims to work out how we might live forever. Bezos had resigned as CEO of Amazon earlier in the year to devote more time to his other ventures, including the aerospace company Blue Origin. He made a short trip into space in July in the company's *New Shepard* rocket. Meanwhile, new laws were passed in California to clamp down on Amazon's use of productivity quotas, which critics say have forced workers to skip bathroom breaks and skirt safety measures.

13 September 2021
Ben Jennings
Guardian

14 September 2021
Steve Bell
Guardian

Work and Pensions Secretary, Therese Coffey, said she was 'entirely happy' with the planned £20 per week cut to Universal Credit. Coffey was then accused of not understanding the scheme after she said that the 'temporary stop-gap' amounted to 'just about two hours of national minimum wage'. The charity Resolution Foundation warned that, due to the taper rate and considering any pension contributions or extra childcare costs, claimants may need to work up to nine extra hours to make up for the cut. Labour called Coffey's comments 'an insult to hard-working families'.

Boris Johnson carried out a major reshuffle of his top team, including firing the education, justice and housing secretaries. Gavin Williamson was removed from the cabinet over his mishandling of school exam results. Dominic Raab was moved from the Foreign Office to the post of justice secretary after receiving much criticism for holidaying during the UK evacuation of Afghanistan. He was also given the title of deputy prime minister amid reports of a heated row over his demotion. Liz Truss replaced Raab to become the Conservative Party's first female foreign secretary.

16 September 2021
Dave Brown
Independent

18 September 2021
Ben Jennings
Guardian

The government announced plans that would allow shops and supermarkets to once again sell goods in imperial weights and measures. The announcement was seen as a largely symbolic move away from EU directives which had standardised the use of metric measurements across the continent. Meanwhile, the UN envoy on poverty warned that the government's plan to cut Universal Credit by £20 per week was an 'unconscionable' move that breached human rights law and failed to protect people from extreme poverty. Olivier De Schutter said that the move was based on a 'very ill-informed understanding' of the impact.

Boris Johnson said that climate talks 'simply must succeed' as Britain prepared to host the COP26 climate summit in Glasgow. The prime minister called on world leaders to be ambitious in their measures to limit global temperature rises to 1.5 degrees and announced that the UK would be one of the first signatories to the Global Methane Pledge, a US and EU initiative to reduce global methane emissions by 30 per cent.

19 September 2021
Nicola Jennings
Guardian

20 September 2021
Brian Adcock
Independent

France recalled its ambassadors to the United States and Australia in a diplomatic row over a submarine deal. It was announced that Australia would be scrapping a $90 billion deal for diesel-powered submarines with France in favour of a new deal to acquire nuclear submarines from the US and UK. The new deal was seen as an attempt by the US to stymie China's dominance in the Pacific but excluded France from any agreement. French foreign minister Jean-Yves Le Drian described the move as a 'stab in the back'.

Boris Johnson was ridiculed for citing Kermit the Frog in a speech to the United Nations General Assembly on climate change. The prime minister said that Kermit was wrong when he sang 'It's Not Easy Bein' Green' because it is, in fact, 'easy, lucrative and right' to be green. One social media user wrote, 'It's official, Boris Johnson's advisers are muppets!' Johnson said that the upcoming COP26 summit must be a 'turning point for humanity' and that humankind must 'grow up' and listen to the warnings of scientists.

25 September 2021
Seamus Jennings
Guardian

27 September 2021
Morten Morland
The Times

Labour's deputy leader Angela Rayner refused to apologise for calling the Conservative government 'scum' at a conference event. Rayner said that she had been using the 'street language' of northern towns and she would only apologise if Boris Johnson also apologised for past remarks that were racist, homophobic and misogynistic. Keir Starmer told the BBC's Andrew Marr that 'Angela and I take a different approach and that is not the language I would have used.'

Thousands of petrol stations ran out of fuel due to panic-buying amid disruption caused by a shortage of truck drivers. Boris Johnson urged motorists to buy fuel in the 'normal way' and said that petrol supplies were 'stabilising' as military tanker drivers were retrained to use civilian fuel tankers. The UK was estimated to be short of more than 100,000 lorry drivers, causing problems for many industries. Meanwhile, the latest James Bond film, *No Time to Die*, had its world premiere at the Royal Albert Hall.

28 September 2021
Christian Adams
Evening Standard

30 September 2021
Steve Bell
Guardian

Keir Starmer faced heckles from Jeremy Corbyn's supporters during his first address as Labour leader at the party conference. Starmer hailed the achievements of New Labour under Tony Blair but attempted to distance himself from Corbyn by pledging to never to go into an election 'with a manifesto that is not a serious plan for government'. He also said that the UK needed an industrial strategy that could encompass robotic technology to free up hospital beds. Starmer had been struggling to shake off what some people saw as his robotic image in comparison to Boris Johnson's larger-than-life personality.

The Conservative government had previously adopted the slogan 'Build Back Better' for its post-Covid-19 recovery plans. Then, in three bizarre videos released on Boris Johnson's Twitter account in October, the prime minister could be seen eating fish and chips, drinking beer and buttering bread – and uttering the punning slogans 'Build Back Batter', 'Build Back Bitter' and 'Build Back Butter', promoting a return to normality. In 2020 the government had initiated its Tackling Obesity strategy, and now it was publicising imminent restrictions on the ways in which unhealthy foodstuffs could be sold and advertised.

5 October 2021
Graeme Bandeira
Yorkshire Post

On 6 October, Boris Johnson closed the Conservative Party conference with a typically jokey and optimistic address, stressing his desire for a 'high-wage economy'. At the same time, the country was experiencing a petrol crisis, caused by panic-buying and a shortage of HGV drivers (which some blamed on Brexit), as well as a rising cost of living and planned rises in National Insurance. A range of commentators, from union leaders to business groups, criticised the speech for being high on feel-good slogans but short on substance, while ignoring realities. The Conservative think-tank Bright Blue concluded: 'The public will soon tire of Boris's banter.'

7 October 2021
Scott Clissold
Daily Telegraph

Beijing sent almost 150 warplanes into Taiwan's air defence zone over four days, marking a sharp escalation in military activity in the region. The Chinese government claims Taiwan as a province of China and has previously vowed to retake it, by force if necessary. Since the 1970s, the United States has followed a 'One China' policy, whereby it recognises the People's Republic of China as the sole sovereign Chinese state while, at the same time, remaining the Republic of Taiwan's most important security ally to deter an attempt at reunification. Following the aerial sorties, Antony Blinken, the US secretary of state, reiterated that America's commitment to Taiwan was 'rock solid'.

8 October 2021
Kevin Kallaugher
Economist

8 October 2021
Christian Adams
Evening Standard

Energy prices soared to unprecedented levels across Europe in response to a natural-gas shortage. The situation was expected to worsen as nations emerged from pandemic slow-downs and headed into winter. Russia, which previously supplied 40 per cent of the European Union's gas, was in the spotlight for failing to deliver the same high volume that it had in pre-pandemic years. This gave rise to accusations that President Putin was effectively turning up the heat on Europe, using Russia's natural resources as a weapon of international coercion. Putin later denied such accusations, calling them 'politically motivated'.

The sale of 80 per cent of Newcastle United FC, for £305 million, to a Saudi investment fund proved controversial. It prompted allegations of greed on the part of the Premier League, which approved the sale, and outcries from Saudi human rights groups. As the cartoonist put it, 'Newcastle United had been taken over by Saudi Arabia's Public Investment Fund, despite concerns over the country's human rights record. But as we all know, the real buyer was Mohammed bin Salman's regime.' Crown Prince Mohammed bin Salman – accused of ordering the murder of journalist Jamal Khashoggi in 2018 – was chair of the fund.

9 October 2021
Peter Brookes
The Times

The Protocol cake in danger

Davey after Gillray

'Everyone has to dig up old James Gillray from time to time,' observed the cartoonist, who reinterpreted Gillray's *The Plumb-pudding in Danger* (1805) to illustrate the rapidly souring relationship between Britain and France over the Northern Ireland Protocol. This Brexit compromise sought to avoid a hard border between the Republic and Northern Ireland by instead establishing an EU/UK customs regime, but Boris Johnson's government now threatened to stymie the protocol if the EU did not agree to renegotiate its terms. According to the cartoonist, the protocol 'had been signed off in 2020 by Boris Johnson without reading it in detail. Emmanuel Macron had eyes on next year's French election and started to rattle his sabre. Johnson just wants cake, lots of it.'

10 October 2021
Andy Davey
Sunday Telegraph

On 14 October, the Queen was overheard in conversation, during the annual opening of the Welsh Parliament, commenting on the upcoming COP26 summit in Glasgow. Expressing some frustration that she still did not 'know who was coming', she also found it 'irritating' that 'they talk but they don't do'. This rare window into the monarch's thoughts made headlines. In 2018, teenage climate activist Greta Thunberg had sat outside the Swedish *Riksdag* (Parliament), arms crossed, in her yellow raincoat, next to a sign calling for a *Skolstrejk för klimatet* – 'school strike for the climate'.

17 October 2021
Morten Morland
The Times

"President Putin can't make it – he's sunning himself in Siberia"

21 October 2021
Steven Camley
Herald Scotland

The Kremlin announced that Vladimir Putin would not be attending the gathering of world leaders at the COP26 climate summit, but no official reason was given. His decision came against a background of very damaging wildfires in the Yakutia province of Siberia, with temperatures reaching 35 degrees. These had come on top of a six-month temperature spike in Siberia during the first half of 2020, which saw the town of Verkhoyansk in the Arctic Circle reach 38 degrees. Putin's decision was seen as a blow to efforts to get world leaders to agree a new deal to stall rising global temperatures.

THE PLAGUE DOCTOR ...

BRING OUT YOUR CONVIVIAL AND FRATERNAL!

Jacob Rees-Mogg, as leader of the House of Commons, faced criticism after saying that Conservative MPs did not need face masks in the House. When challenged about the paucity of Conservative MPs wearing masks – despite rising numbers of Covid-19 infections – Rees-Mogg asserted: 'The advice on crowded spaces refers to crowded spaces with people that you don't know. We on this side know each other ... we on this side have a more convivial fraternal spirit and are following the advice of Her Majesty's Government.' Yet Health Secretary Sajid Javid was at the same time recommending mask-wearing as a useful precaution for the public.

23 October 2021
Dave Brown
Independent

On 26 October, the government amended its Environment Bill. Previously, Conservative MPs had rejected a House of Lords amendment placing legal obligations on water companies to stop releasing untreated sewage into waterways: Boris Johnson had protested that such measures would cost £150 billion and it was 'not right to sign a blank cheque on behalf of customers'. Yet a popular outcry forced a rapid U-turn. The government now promised a legally binding 'progressive reduction in the adverse impacts from storm overflows', which would require water companies to reduce sewage overspills.

27 October 2021
Graeme Bandeira
Yorkshire Post

When Chancellor Rishi Sunak revealed his autumn budget, he proclaimed 'historically high levels of public spending'. Higher than expected forecasts of 6.5 per cent economic growth lay behind a raft of headline measures, such as £150 billion of extra spending for government departments. The *Telegraph* journalist and GB News economics editor Liam Halligan declared that 'this was a budget that Gordon Brown could have given', in reference to the former Labour chancellor and prime minister. Others demurred, pointing to rising prices, an imminent increase in National Insurance and looming hikes in energy bills.

28 October 2021
Patrick Blower
Daily Telegraph

30 October 2021
Rebecca Hendin
Guardian

Just before Halloween, Facebook founder Mark Zuckerberg announced that his company would be changing its name to 'Meta'. In a presentation at the company's annual Connect conference, Zuckerberg revealed his plans to create a 'metaverse', which he described as 'an embodied internet where you're in the experience, not just looking at it'. He conceived of it as a place where 'you're going to able to do almost anything you can imagine'. Zuckerberg's dream of super-enhanced virtual reality struck some as *Alice-in-Wonderland*-like escapism from the world's problems.

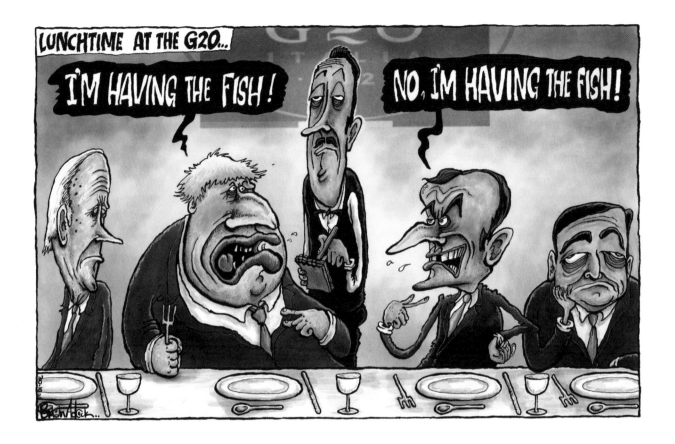

French President Emmanuel Macron exacerbated the Anglo-French dispute over fishing rights by questioning the UK's 'credibility' and accusing Boris Johnson of flouting existing agreements. The Brexit terms had allowed for continued fishing by British trawlers operating in EU waters, and vice versa. But deciding which boats should receive licences became a contentious issue. A Scottish trawler was impounded in Le Havre for fishing 'illegally', and Macron threatened retaliatory measures if the UK did not grant more fishing licences. Johnson vowed to do 'whatever was necessary' to protect British fishermen and to impose 'rigorous checks' on foreign vessels.

30 October 2021
Brian Adcock
Independent

As world leaders at COP26 signed a declaration on forests and land use, US President Joe Biden told them that 'conserving our forests and other critical ecosystems is indispensable'. However, Biden attracted criticism due to the sheer size of the entourage he was travelling with and its carbon footprint. On 29 October, while at the G20 summit in Rome, Biden's visit to the Pope had necessitated an 85-car motorcade, because of Italian social-distancing rules. Biden travelled in his 20,000-pound armoured Cadillac called 'The Beast', which was reported to manage just 8 miles per gallon. His journey from Edinburgh to COP26 in Glasgow involved a mere 21 vehicles.

2 November 2021
Steven Camley
Herald Scotland

On 1 November, Boris Johnson welcomed more than 120 world leaders to the COP26 summit in Glasgow. At the same time, protest actions were under way in the city as climate activists expressed deep scepticism about the conference's chances of generating meaningful change. Greta Thunberg told young activists at the 'Fridays for Future' event, just outside the COP26 venue, that 'change is not going to come from inside there', because the politicians were just 'pretending to take our future seriously'. It was, in her view, just more 'blah, blah, blah'.

2 November 2021
Brian Adcock
Independent

Two hundred and forty-eight Conservative MPs, backed by Boris Johnson, narrowly voted through Andrea Leadsom's amendment which, in effect, reprieved Conservative backbencher Owen Paterson from a 30-day suspension from the House of Commons. Previously, the Parliamentary Committee on Standards had concluded that Paterson had repeatedly breached rules by lobbying ministers on behalf of two companies who were paying him more than £100,000. Jacob Rees-Mogg supported the amendment and questioned the committee's treatment of Paterson. Chris Bryant, a Labour MP and chair of the standards committee, said the amendment 'would create a special system for one person and is completely unfair'.

4 November 2021
Steven Camley
Herald Scotland

So fierce was the backlash over the Leadsom amendment, which would scrap the Committee on Standards in favour of a Conservative-led watchdog, that within 24 hours there was a government U-turn: the new committee was scrapped, and another vote would be held to determine the fate of Owen Paterson. Accusations also emerged that Conservative MPs had been threatened with the loss of local funding unless they voted for the amendment. In response, Labour leader Keir Starmer said that the prime minister was 'corrupt' and 'in the sewer with his troops'. Amid the furore, Paterson resigned as an MP, blaming the 'cruel world of politics'.

7 November 2021
Chris Riddell
Observer

12 November 2021
Steve Bell
Guardian

Despite a government announcement in September of an extra £36 billion to be spent on health and social care over three years, new data from NHS England confirmed that more than 5.8 million people were waiting for their hospital treatment to begin – a rise of more than 1 million in a year. More than 350,000 of them had been for waiting over a year. Matthew Taylor, chief executive of NHS Confederation, explained that emergency admissions were preventing progress on the backlog and that '90,000-plus vacancies' in NHS staff meant that it was not possible to 'buy our way out of this potential crisis'.

As the COP26 summit considered the threats to low-lying islands from climate change, Conservative MPs' outside interests were in the spotlight again. Footage showed Sir Geoffrey Cox taking part in a virtual hearing from his parliamentary office, but as part of his private legal role for the British Virgin Islands. MPs are not permitted to use parliamentary resources for outside work. Furthermore, it was revealed that Cox had visited the Caribbean in April, May and June, during which time he had taken part in Commons votes by proxy. The parliamentary commissioner for standards eventually declined to investigate. Cox's fees for this work were reputedly upwards of £900,000.

13 November 2021
Ben Jennings
Guardian

In the first months of 2021, large numbers of Russian troops had been deployed to the border with Ukraine, as Vladimir Putin ratcheted up tensions with the neighbouring state. Although there was a notional Russian withdrawal in April, by mid-November satellite images confirmed the existence of another build-up, put at 100,000 Russian soldiers with their military hardware. NATO's secretary-general warned of 'an unusual concentration of troops'. In the cartoonist's eyes, 'Inscrutable Vladimir Putin was testing the engine as he amassed Russian military forces at the Ukraine border . . . The Russian premier continued to deny intentions to invade.'

13 November 2021
Andy Davey
Daily Telegraph

"Hold it – no entry without proof of two jobs."

Controversy over MPs' jobs outside Parliament continued to haunt the government in the wake of the Paterson and Cox affairs. On 17 November, Conservative MPs voted down a Labour motion banning MPs from being paid as 'political' consultants. Instead, a government-backed amendment passed, keeping MPs' roles outside Parliament to 'reasonable limits' – yet to be defined. According to the *Guardian*, a quarter of Conservative MPs (90) held second jobs, around half of them as consultants, compared to nine MPs holding second jobs from across the Labour, Liberal Democrat and Scottish National parties.

18 November 2021
Steven Camley
Herald Scotland

Transport Secretary Grant Shapps revealed that the government was scrapping the eastern arm of the HS2 high-speed rail link (connecting Birmingham and Leeds) and the fast Northern Powerhouse Rail line connecting Leeds, Bradford and Manchester, as part of a new Integrated Rail Plan. HS2's western arm would still connect London to Manchester, via Birmingham. While Shapps claimed that the new focus on other rail projects and upgrades to existing lines would mean faster progress towards quicker journeys, his Labour opposite number called the decision a 'great train robbery'; others called it a 'betrayal' of the North.

19 November 2021
Paul Thomas
Daily Mail

Despite threats of a rebellion, Conservative MPs narrowly backed Boris Johnson's plan to exclude means-tested state support from the new £86,000 lifetime cap on how much individuals pay towards their social care costs. The original plan was for the cap to account for both care costs paid by individuals and contributions from councils. Conservative backbencher Damien Green called the move 'monstrously unfair', because those owning houses in poorer areas were 'more likely' to have to sell their properties than homeowners in wealthier areas with higher house values.

23 November 2021
Morten Morland
The Times

23 November 2021
Patrick Blower
Daily Telegraph

Having lost his place in a speech to the Confederation of British Industry on 22 November, Boris Johnson began a digression about a theme park devoted to a children's TV character. 'Yesterday I went, as we all must, to Peppa Pig World,' he uttered, which was 'very much my kind of place' with its 'very safe streets', 'discipline in schools' and 'heavy emphasis on mass transit systems'. The somewhat surreal ad-libbing came after a long pause, as he asked his audience repeatedly to 'forgive me' and shuffled his papers, before navigating back to his theme of private-sector creativity and innovation in the UK.

On 24 November, a flimsy dinghy carrying migrants to the UK capsized in French waters. Twenty-seven people died – most of those on board – making it the worst death toll to date in the burgeoning people-smuggling crisis. Boris Johnson emphasised a determination to 'break these gangs that are literally getting away with murder', as the government implied that French authorities were not doing enough to interrupt the smuggling rackets. The cartoon alludes to the Book of Exodus, in which God parts the waves for Moses and the Israelites to escape across the Red Sea before the waters drown the pursuing Egyptians.

28 November 2021
Seamus Jennings
Guardian

29 November 2021
Brian Adcock
Independent

Boris Johnson confirmed new Covid-19 'targeted measures' following evidence that two cases of the new Omicron variant (with its multiple mutations in spike proteins) had been identified in Essex and Nottingham. A rapid rise in infections in South Africa had been attributed to the new variant, although it had now reached as far as Hong Kong and Israel, as well as Europe. Early indications suggested that Omicron was more transmissible than the longer-established Delta variant. However, the government reiterated the view of 'experts' that the existing vaccines would provide 'protection against the new variant'.

The spread of the Omicron variant drew attention to the fact that South Africa had achieved only a 27-per-cent vaccination rate, while rates in much of the developing world were considerably lower. Parliamentarians had told Boris Johnson that he had a 'moral duty' to donate one dose abroad for every vaccine administered in the UK, and Conservative backbenchers pressured him to boost supplies to countries with a 'desperate shortage'. In June 2021, the G7 nations had pledged to donate 1 billion doses, yet distribution lagged behind. In the *Guardian*, Gordon Brown wrote, 'Only when we reject vaccine nationalism and medical protectionism will we stop outbreaks becoming pandemics.'

29 November 2021
Nicola Jennings
Guardian

30 November 2021
Christian Adams
Evening Standard

Multiple news outlets described Labour deputy leader Angela Rayner as 'blindsided' when Keir Starmer's second reshuffle of his shadow cabinet overshadowed a speech she was giving to the Institute of Government. It appeared that she had not been informed of Starmer's timing and, in awkward press interviews, said she did not 'know the details of any reshuffle' and 'we need some consistency in how we're approaching things as an opposition'. Meanwhile, the government reimposed mandatory mask-wearing on public transport and in shops in response to a rise in cases of the Omicron variant.

In the electoral battleground of the Old Bexley and Sidcup by-election, both main parties claimed their own victory. The Conservatives held the safe seat, which had become vacant on the death of James Brokenshire. They won 51 per cent of votes, but low turnout contributed to a near 19,000 majority being slashed to 4,478 votes. Labour could claim a 10-per-cent swing to them and the highest vote share in 20 years – along with the observation that the prime minister would lose his Uxbridge and South Ruislip seat if such a swing were replicated there.

3 December 2021
Christian Adams
Evening Standard

Britain's largest private-sector union, Unite, announced that it would slash its political donations and redirect money to various social and economic campaigns instead. The union had been the biggest financial backer of the Labour Party but would now pay only 'affiliation fees' of £1 million on the grounds that the party 'needs to defend workers'. The cartoonist commented: 'Soon after being elected general secretary of Unite, Sharon Graham declared her intention to get combative with Starmer's middle-ground, lacklustre Labour . . . The Red Wall had already been demolished, what further pain could she cause him?'

4 December 2021
Andy Davey
Daily Telegraph

Footage emerged of a mock press conference from 22 December 2020, in which Allegra Stratton – Boris Johnson's press secretary at the time – joked with colleagues about a Downing Street party that broke lockdown rules. It proved fatal to her government role. On 8 December 2021, the former journalist told press that she was resigning to avoid becoming a 'distraction' from the battle against Covid-19, and she tearfully apologised for seeming to make light of 'rules that people were doing everything to obey'.

9 December 2021
Steven Camley
Herald Scotland

10 December 2021
Andy Davey
Daily Telegraph

Allegra Stratton's resignation did not draw a line under 'Partygate'. As rumours of other parties swirled, and questions were asked about whether politicians had attended them, a beleaguered Boris Johnson announced a civil service investigation into the matter, to be conducted by Sue Gray. According to the cartoonist, 'Reports of seven alleged parties held the previous Christmas across government had emerged after the initial report of just one or two having taken place. Meanwhile Health Secretary Sajid Javid warned that the NHS might be "completely overwhelmed" since the number of Omicron variant cases was doubling every 2.5 to 3 days.'

The prime minister's wife, Carrie Johnson, who had once been the Conservative Party's head of communications, gave birth to a baby girl on 9 December. According to the cartoonist, '2021 could not have ended much worse for Boris Johnson. He was fighting fires on every front, from illegal parties in Number 10 to sleaze allegations, after an investigation concluded he had asked a Tory donor to find extra cash to refurbish his Downing Street flat. The arrival of his and Carrie's second child – and *his* umpteenth – arguably couldn't have come at a better time.'

10 December 2021
Peter Brookes
The Times

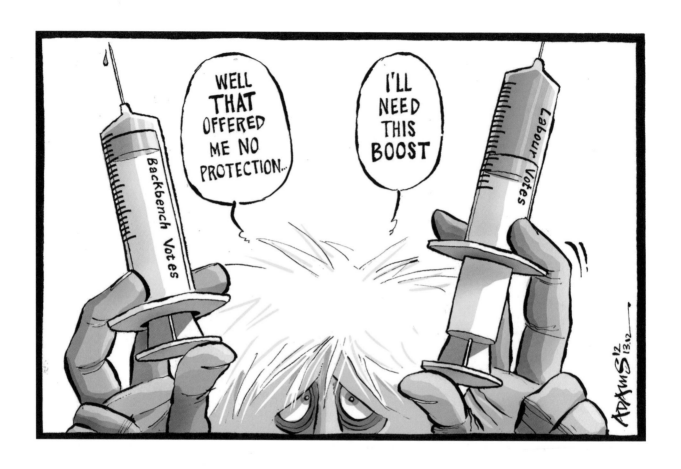

14 December 2021
Christian Adams
Evening Standard

As Sajid Javid warned MPs about the threat from rapidly rising cases of the Omicron variant, MPs voted on 14 December on whether to approve the introduction of 'vaccine certificates'. If the measures were voted through, evidence of vaccination would become mandatory to gain entry to larger venues such as nightclubs. Boris Johnson's government won the day, by 239 votes; but humiliatingly, he had to rely on Labour votes. In the biggest backbench rebellion since Johnson became prime minister, 99 Conservatives voted with the 'noes', while another 35 Conservatives abstained.

Justice Secretary Dominic Raab launched a three-month consultation on his proposals to replace the Human Rights Act 1998 with a bill of rights. He had claimed that the 'typically British' changes would bring a 'healthy dose of common sense'. Eye-catching elements included making claimants pass a stage of 'permission' before pursuing a human rights claim in the courts, and reining in Article 8 of the current act – involving rights to family life – to make deportation easier. Critics saw the proposals as strengthening government over the individual, and the human rights group Liberty called them 'a blatant, unashamed power grab'.

15 December 2021
Dave Brown
Independent

ISSUES ON THE DOORSTEP...

When Helen Morgan won the constituency of North Shropshire on 16 December for the Liberal Democrats, it sent shockwaves through the Conservative Party. The by-election in the once rock-solid Conservative seat was necessitated by Owen Paterson's resignation. In a relatively high turnout, the Conservative majority of 23,000 was replaced by a Liberal Democrat majority of nearly 6,000. During a sometimes tetchy post-election interview, Boris Johnson complained about others – seeming to imply the media – focusing on a 'litany of stuff' and 'questions about politics and politicians' that were distracting from the government's successes.

17 December 2021
Ben Jennings
i

In the aftermath of the North Shropshire by-election, the revelations about Partygate and the rebellion by Conservative MPs over vaccine certificates, Boris Johnson's prime ministership looked imperilled. The prime minister faced a further rebellion when almost 100 Conservative MPs voted against plans to introduce Plan B Covid restrictions, which included mandatory face masks in shops and on public transport, and compulsory vaccination for NHS workers. The motion only passed due to Labour votes. In the words of the cartoonist, 'Boris faced revolt from Tory MPs over Plan B restrictions' and now there were 'rumours they are having "conversations" about how to oust him. His time may be short.'

17 December 2021
Andy Davey
Jewish Chronicle

Boris Johnson's isolation seemed ever greater when it emerged that his Brexit minister, Lord Frost, had quit. His resignation letter alluded to 'concerns about the directions of travel' and to hopes that Johnson would not be 'tempted by the kind of coercive measures we have seen elsewhere' in response to Covid-19. The resignation shocked members of a Conservative WhatsApp group called 'Clean Global Brexit', who described the resignation as a 'disaster' for the prime minister. Culture Secretary Nadine Dorries, a notable Johnson loyalist, was removed from the group for replying that the prime minister was a 'hero'.

20 December 2021
Brian Adcock
Independent

Following denials of a Downing Street party said to have occurred on 15 May 2020, the press published a leaked picture of Boris Johnson, with his then-fiancée Carrie and their new baby, sharing cheese and wine with staff in the Number 10 garden. The prime minister asserted that it showed 'people at work, talking about work', while Keir Starmer highlighted the contrast with those unable to attend their loved ones' funerals at the time. On that same day in May 2020, Health Secretary Matt Hancock had cautioned the public not to gather socially in the good weather.

21 December 2021
Morten Morland
The Times

A noticeable divergence emerged between Boris Johnson's message that planned pre-Christmas events and social gatherings should go ahead and the much more cautious approach of England's chief medical officer, Sir Chris Whitty. At a government Covid-19 briefing, Whitty urged people not to mix with 'people you don't have to'. Many were already heeding that advice, with the hospitality industry complaining of a 'lockdown by stealth'. On Twitter, Conservative MP Joy Morrissey opined that 'the unelected Covid public health spokesperson' should defer to elected politicians. 'This is not a public health socialist state,' she wrote.

23 December 2021
Graeme Bandeira
Yorkshire Post

DAVID SIMONDS 24.12.21.

By late December, scientists around the world were beginning to conclude that the Omicron variant was generally milder than the Delta variant, in that there was a substantially lower risk (by 30–70 per cent) of an infection necessitating hospital admission. This finding was of little comfort to hospitals under pressure, though, for it appeared that Omicron's 'mildness' was cancelled out by its much greater ease of transmission. As Christmas approached, 94.5 per cent of English NHS hospital beds were occupied – 5.5 per cent more than in the pre-vaccine December of 2020.

24 December 2021
David Simonds
Independent

27 December 2021
Brian Adcock
Independent

Christmas Day 2021 brought the highest daily tally of Covid-19 cases to date in England, at 113,638, as well as the highest daily number of hospital admissions in ten months. Scotland, Northern Ireland and Wales were already reintroducing social distancing and restrictions on social gatherings. Boris Johnson was set to receive a full briefing from Chris Whitty and the government's chief scientific adviser, Sir Patrick Vallance. The image evokes the poster from Tim Burton's 1993 animated fantasy, *The Nightmare Before Christmas*.

The verdict in a New York court that Ghislaine Maxwell, the former associate of the late Jeffrey Epstein, was guilty of grooming and sex trafficking increased pressure on Prince Andrew. A civil suit launched against him by Virginia Giuffre alleged that she had been groomed by Maxwell and, at age 17, had been pressed into having sex with the prince three times. During a November 2019 interview with the BBC's Emily Maitlis, Prince Andrew had denied meeting Giuffre. He had dismissed her claim that he sweated on the dance floor with the assertion that an adrenaline spike during his Falklands War experience had left him 'unable to sweat'.

31 December 2021
Morten Morland
The Times

Keir Starmer used his first major speech of 2022 to put patriotism at the forefront of Labour's strategy. He described Labour's mission as being to 'extend security, prosperity and respect to all', which, Starmer insisted, expressed the nature of a 'deeply patriotic party'. Starmer also looked forward to the Queen's Platinum Jubilee and the Commonwealth Games and claimed that it was 'precisely because we are patriotic' that Labour criticised things that were going wrong in the country. This patriotic emphasis was already controversial with some senior MPs on the party's left.

5 January 2022
Dave Brown
Independent

One year after the failed insurrection to overturn the results of the 2020 US presidential election, commentators reflected that Donald Trump's hold on the Republican Party seemed stronger than ever. Political analyst David Schultz told *Al Jazeera* that 'The Republican Party is Trump now.' The former president was assiduously endorsing his favoured candidates for the mid-term congressional elections, and his fundraising efforts were matching those of the party itself – all in spite of continuing legal imbroglios surrounding the Capitol Hill riots and investigations into his tax affairs. The traditional symbol of the Republican Party is an elephant, shown here being swallowed whole.

7 January 2022
Kevin Kallaugher
Economist

In June 2020, protestors in Bristol had torn down a statue of slave trader Edward Colston, resulting in prosecutions for criminal damage. In January 2022, four of the accused were acquitted, after successfully claiming that the statue constituted a hate crime. Some politicians were unimpressed. Grant Shapps spoke of a 'loophole' in the law that the new Police, Crime, Sentencing and Courts Bill would close. Robert Jenrick tweeted that accepting 'vandalism and criminal damage' would 'undermine the rule of law'.

10 January 2022
Ben Jennings
Guardian

When tennis star Novak Djokovic landed in Melbourne on 5 January 2022 to defend his Australian Open title, he did so under a medical exemption (reviewed by a panel of experts appointed by the Australian government) from the strict rule that all arrivals should be vaccinated against Covid-19. Unimpressed border authorities detained him in a hotel, while the federal government cancelled his visa. However, on 10 January a successful legal appeal saw Djokovic's right of entry restored. Six days later, three federal judges confirmed the immigration minister's use of 'discretionary' powers to cancel the sportsman's visa – and Djokovic was swiftly deported.

11 January 2022
Brian Adcock
Independent

DAVID SIMONDS 14.1.22

The *Daily Telegraph* revealed that two leaving parties had taken place at Downing Steet on 16 April 2021 and had eventually merged in the garden of Number 10, with attendees staying and drinking into the night. The day after, and in strict compliance with Covid-19 restrictions on gatherings, the Queen had sat alone for the funeral of her husband of 73 years, the Duke of Edinburgh. As the cartoonist put it, 'I contrasted the mass partying at 10 Downing Street with the behaviour of the Queen who was mourning the death of Prince Philip on her own.'

14 January 2022
David Simonds
Evening Standard

ONE SON GALOOT

When, on 12 January, a New York judge allowed Virginia Giuffre's civil case against Prince Andrew to proceed, there was a swift reaction from the monarchy. Within hours, a Buckingham Palace statement confirmed that 'The Duke of York's military affiliations and Royal patronages have been returned to the Queen.' Furthermore, 'The Duke of York will continue not to undertake any public duties and is defending the case as a private citizen.' These decisions entailed Andrew's loss of the title 'His Royal Highness'. There was speculation that princes Charles and William had demanded an uncompromising response to protect the reputation of the monarchy and Royal Family.

15 January 2022
Dave Brown
Independent

15 January 2022
Ben Jennings

i

On 11 January, Boris Johnson admitted to Parliament that he had attended a Downing Street garden party on 20 May 2020 in order to 'thank groups of staff'. While acknowledging that 'with hindsight' he should have asked attendees to go back inside, he also insisted that he 'believed implicitly that this was a work event'. That justification attracted ridicule and incredulity from beyond the political opposition. The event had taken place after Johnson's principal private secretary, Martin Reynolds, had sent an email inviting more than 100 colleagues to 'socially distanced drinks', telling them to 'bring your own booze'.

Nadine Dorries announced that the BBC would need to find an alternative source of funding as the TV licence fee was to be frozen for the next two years and abolished from 2028. However, when announcing the policy in Parliament the next day, Dorries insisted that no decision had been made on the future of the licence fee – leaving some to speculate that her provocative announcement had been designed to distract from Partygate. The cartoon mimics the Test Card – the static image used on the BBC for decades when no programme was being broadcast, in which a little girl played noughts and crosses. In this case, the cartoonist replaced the accompanying doll, 'Bubbles', with a Boris Johnson-like rag doll.

16 January 2022
Christian Adams
Evening Standard

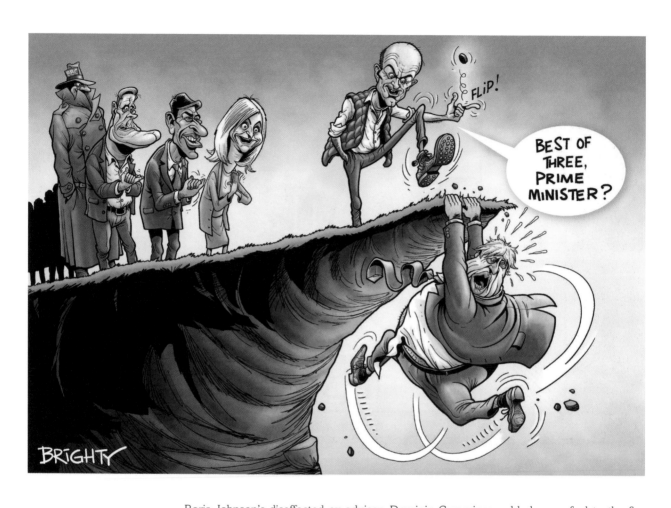

FLIP!

BEST OF THREE, PRIME MINISTER?

BRIGHTY

17 January 2022
Steve Bright
Sun

Boris Johnson's disaffected ex-adviser, Dominic Cummings, added more fuel to the fire surrounding the Downing Street garden party on 20 May 2020. He rubbished the prime minister's claims not to have known details of the event in advance, claiming that some senior civil servants had queried the advisability and legality of the invitation from Martin Reynolds, who had replied that he would check with the prime minister. If true, Cummings' allegations suggested Johnson had lied to Parliament.

As controversy deepened over Partygate, the newspapers were rife with reports of 'pork pie' plotters – nervous Conservative MPs in Red Wall constituencies, who wanted to see a leadership election. In 2012, while mayor of London, Johnson had found himself dangling inelegantly from a zip line during a publicity stunt. According to the cartoonist, Johnson, 'hanging from a zip line like a piñata (which only happened because he lied about his weight to the zip-wire safety guys) is threatened by familiar members of the cabinet, none of whom could land a blow, and the greased piglet lived to fart another day'.

20 January 2022
Guy Venables
Metro

20 January 2022
Steven Camley
Herald Scotland

Following an interview in which Boris Johnson told Sky News that 'nobody told me' the alleged parties were against Covid-19 rules, his situation became ever more precarious. On 19 January, minutes before Prime Minister's Questions opened in Parliament, Christian Wakeford – Conservative MP for Bury South – defected to Labour. And during a noisy PMQs, the senior Conservative backbencher David Davis invoked the blunt phrase used both by Oliver Cromwell and against Prime Minister Neville Chamberlain in 1940: 'In the name of God, go!' It all had the whiff of Shakespearean drama.

Conservative MP Nusrat Ghani claimed that, in 2020, the chief whip had informed her that her sacking as transport minister was in part because her 'Muslimness was raised as an issue' at Downing Street. The whip, revealed as Mark Spencer, flatly denied the conversation. Meanwhile, Boris Johnson said he took the allegation 'extremely seriously', though his 2018 description of Muslim women in burkas as looking 'like letterboxes' was a matter of record. The late comedian Ken Dodd, with his distinctive tickling-stick prop, had a hit 1964 song with the lyrics 'Happiness!/ Happiness!/ The greatest gift/ that I possess.'

25 January 2022
Steve Bell
Guardian

26 January 2022
Patrick Blower
Daily Telegraph

On 25 January, the Metropolitan Police reversed its position on investigating possible lockdown breaches and announced it would now look into 'alleged gatherings on government premises' on eight dates between May 2020 and April 2021. One of these was a supposed Downing Street party on 19 June 2020 for Boris Johnson's birthday, at which he had been presented with a cake. Northern Ireland Minister Conor Burns attempted to extricate the prime minister from culpability on the basis that he had been 'in a sense, ambushed by a cake'.

In August 2021, during the Taliban reconquest of Kabul, the evacuation of a planeload of dogs and other animals belonging to the animal charity Nowzad led to claims that animals were being prioritised above people. There were accusations that the prime minister had personally intervened to help the charity's head, ex-Royal Marine Pen Farthing, get clearance for the flight. Johnson denied 'influence on that particular case', but the row erupted again in late January 2022, when a leaked Foreign Office email included the phrase 'the PM has just authorised their staff and animals to be evacuated.' The charity's staff were not flown out.

27 January 2022
Steven Camley
Herald Scotland

29 January 2022
Ben Jennings
i

Scotland Yard was forced to deny that the Metropolitan Police was hindering Sue Gray's inquiry into alleged parties at Downing Street, after it asked her to make 'minimal reference' to the specific events they were also looking into. Gray was preparing to release a report following her internal investigation into the parties, but parts of it would now have to be redacted, and the publication of the full report delayed, in order to avoid 'prejudice' in the Met's enquiries. Sceptics were concerned that the delay offered the prime minister some breathing space.

Boris Johnson warned Vladimir Putin to 'step back from the brink' in advance of his trip to Ukraine. The prime minister said any invasion of Ukraine would be 'an absolute disaster for the world'. Russia had amassed 120,000 troops on the Ukrainian border and was stockpiling supplies to treat casualties, increasing fears of an imminent invasion. Earlier in the month, the prime minister had apologised for attending gatherings during lockdown. He repeatedly claimed that he did not know the events were against the rules because he believed them to be work events.

31 January 2022
Morten Morland
The Times

THE GREAT LEVELLER

SCHOOL

The North ›

2 February 2022
Christian Adams
Evening Standard

Michael Gove defended the government's Levelling Up White Paper, aimed at addressing social and economic disparities across the UK. Its four 'objectives' included a 'fundamental rewiring' to boost productivity and opportunity, and to strengthen communities and local powers. Gove said that 'too much' had been spent on London and now 'we're making sure in Wolverhampton, in Sheffield and in other areas that we put our money where our mouth is'. London's *Evening Standard* pointed out that the city had some of the 'deepest pockets of deprivation in the country'.

Many feared that Sue Gray's report on Partygate would be heavily redacted, in compliance with the Metropolitan Police's wishes that she did not prejudice their enquiries. In the event, the document released on 31 January was a 12-page summary mentioning no individuals. Billed as an 'Update' pending release of the full report, it concluded: 'a number of these gatherings should not have been allowed to take place or to develop in the way that they did.' In Parliament, Boris Johnson said 'sorry' and announced a shake-up of the Downing Street machine. (*Fifty Shades of Grey* was the 2011 erotic bestseller by E.L. James, which spawned a film franchise.)

2 February 2022
Steve Bright
Sun

"Gentlemen, he needs to go. We've just received three letters of No Confidence and the Gas bill."

The growing discontent among Conservatives ramped up when three backbenchers – Sir Gary Streeter, Tobias Ellwood and Anthony Mangnall – submitted letters of no-confidence in Boris Johnson's leadership to the chair of Conservative MPs' 1922 Committee. Streeter opined that he could not 'reconcile the pain and sacrifice of the vast majority of the British public during lockdown' with the behaviour of 'those working in Downing Street'. At the same time, the energy regulator, Ofgem, announced that the price cap for consumers' gas and electricity bills would rise by 54 per cent on 1 April.

3 February 2022
Steven Camley
Herald Scotland

As Ofgem confirmed that the average annual domestic energy bill would soon soar to £1,915, new figures revealed the sheer cost to the nation's coffers of sub-standard and over-priced contracts for personal protective equipment (PPE) in the battle against Covid-19. The *Daily Mail* called this £8.7 billion spend a 'staggering illustration of government waste'. Moreover, the National Audit Office calculated that the difference between the high prices paid for PPE and the low value of unused and outdated stockpiles represented a loss of £4.7 billion. Under pressure in Parliament, Rishi Sunak promised that any cases of fraud would be investigated.

4 February 2022
Morten Morland
The Times

Although Boris Johnson had promised to reform Downing Street following Sue Gray's 'Update', he was plagued by a spate of resignations. He lost his chief of staff, Dan Rosenfield, along with his principal private secretary, Martin Reynolds, who had issued the now-infamous email invitation to the 'bring your own booze' event in May 2020. The Number 10 director of communications, Jack Doyle, also departed, as did longtime aide Munira Mirza, whose patience with Johnson snapped over his recent (inaccurate) gibe that Keir Starmer had failed to prosecute paedophile Jimmy Savile when director of public prosecutions.

4 February 2022
David Simonds
Evening Standard

As alarm bells continued to sound over Russia's intentions towards Ukraine, Emmanuel Macron visited Moscow for several hours of man-to-man talks with Vladimir Putin. The cartoon evokes two historic references: the Fontainbleau-school painting *Gabrielle d'Estrées and One of Her Sisters*, for the nipple-tweaking, and the French Romantic painter Ernest Meissonier, among whose heroic subjects was Napoleon Bonaparte on horseback. The visuals of the actual Macron–Putin summit were notable not for any displays of macho intimacy, but rather for the massive white table creating a gulf between them. Following the meeting, Macron warned that 'the risk of destabilisation is increasing.'

8 February 2022
Steve Bell
Guardian

In politics, the so-called 'dead cat' ploy is a way of avoiding an uncomfortable discussion by means of a dramatic but irrelevant distraction – such as throwing a dead cat on the table. After Boris Johnson falsely accused Keir Starmer of 'failing' to prosecute Jimmy Savile when Starmer was director of public prosecutions, the prime minister refused to apologise for what Starmer called a 'ridiculous slur'. Later, Johnson claimed he was not referring to Starmer's 'personal record'. Starmer was subsequently mobbed by angry protestors who accused him of 'protecting paedophiles' and had to be bundled into his car by police officers.

9 February 2022
Dave Brown
Independent

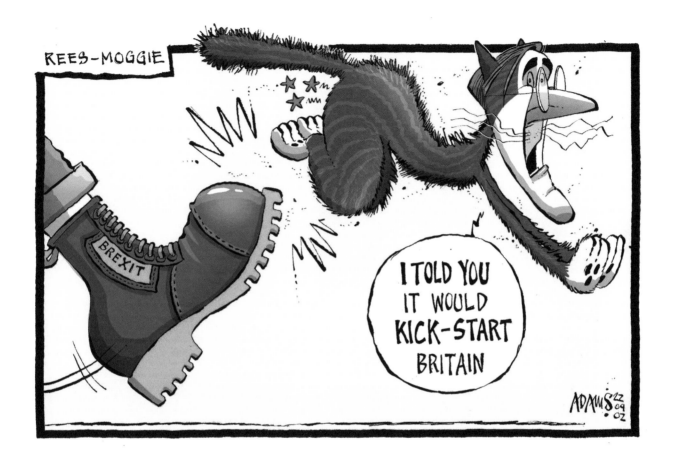

Boris Johnson made Jacob Rees-Mogg a full member of the cabinet as the 'Minister for Brexit Opportunities and Government Efficiency'. The appointment was mocked on Twitter by the Belgian MEP Guy Verhofstadt, who said: 'Surrealism is tasking a man who said the benefits of Brexit wouldn't be known for 50 years to deliver them now!' Meanwhile, footage emerged of West Ham United footballer Kurt Zouma kicking his Bengal cat across the kitchen floor. His club immediately fined him, and a court later convicted him of unnecessary cruelty to an animal.

9 February 2022
Christian Adams
Evening Standard

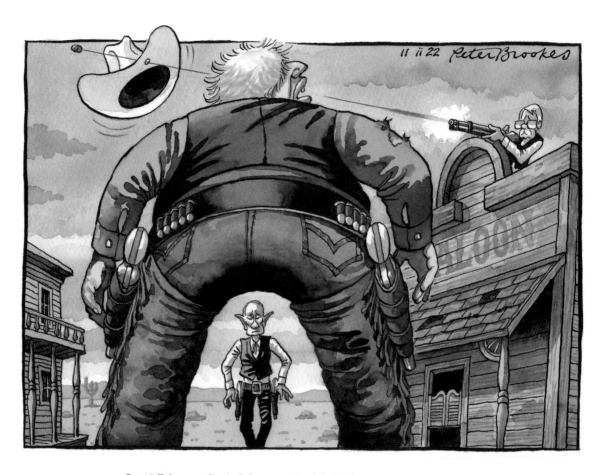

On 10 February, Boris Johnson visited Poland to meet with his Polish counterpart, Mateusz Morawiecki. As fears over Putin's intentions towards Ukraine grew, Johnson proclaimed that 'Poland and the UK won't accept a world in which a powerful neighbour can bully or attack their neighbours.' On the same day, ex-prime minister John Major offered excoriating criticism of Johnson in a speech to the Institute of Government. Major said that Johnson 'broke lockdown laws', viewed the truth as 'optional' and made the government 'look distinctly shifty'.

11 February 2022
Peter Brookes
The Times

While several Western countries offered to send weapons to Ukraine to strengthen its defence capabilities in the event of a Russian invasion, Germany's promise of a mere 5,000 helmets drew derision. The German defence minister, Christine Lambrecht, tried to sell the offer as a 'very clear signal' of German support for Ukraine. By contrast, the celebrity mayor of Kyiv, ex-boxer Vitali Klitschko, concluded that the offer was 'an absolute joke'. He wondered what Germany would send next: 'pillows?' In the past, inadequately resourced German troops had reportedly had to train with brooms instead of guns.

14 February 2022
Patrick Blower
Daily Telegraph

The prospect of Prince Andrew testifying over the allegations from Virginia Giuffre vanished when the Duke of York offered an undisclosed sum to settle the case – without any admission of guilt. The next day, Prince Charles and his staff were in the spotlight, as the Metropolitan Police announced it would investigate the alleged promise of a knighthood and British citizenship to a Saudi billionaire in exchange for financial support for The Prince's Foundation. The 1992 Disney film *Aladdin* contained the song 'A Whole New World', sung on a swirling magic carpet.

18 February 2022
Rebecca Hendin
Guardian

As the Winter Olympic Games in Beijing drew to a close, President Biden warned that he was 'convinced' Vladimir Putin would imminently invade Ukraine. Despite Russian protestations to the contrary, the Russian build-up of military forces on the Ukrainian and Belarusian borders had continued. A particular concern was that Russia would mount a 'false-flag' operation, deploying its own forces in Ukrainian guise, to manufacture a pretext for invasion. Meanwhile, across the UK, Storm Eunice blew in – the second major storm in three days. It prompted a red weather warning across southern England.

20 February 2022
Chris Riddell
Observer

THE END OF LEGAL RESTRICTIONS...

THE CLINICALLY VULNERABLE

FORGET ABOUT PARTYGATE

THE   OLD

22 February 2022
Brian Adcock
Independent

Under its 'learning to live with Covid' policy, Boris Johnson's government confirmed on 21 February that vaccines would remain the 'first line of defence' against the disease and announced the imminent removal of all Covid-related rules, including the need to self-isolate after a 'positive' test. Some critics highlighted the potential risk to the clinically vulnerable. And among those testing positive, just a few days earlier, was the nearly 96-year-old Queen. Buckingham Palace confirmed that she was suffering from 'mild, cold-like symptoms' but would be monitored.

The official recognition by Russia of the two pro-Moscow, breakaway regions of eastern Ukraine as the independent 'Luhansk People's Republic' and the 'Donetsk People's Republic' was accompanied by the promise of sending Russian 'peacekeeping' forces there. The NATO secretary-general, Jens Stoltenberg, condemned the move, as did an array of Western and EU leaders including Biden and Johnson, who began to announce sanctions against Russian interests and the breakaway 'republics'. Meanwhile, Russian tanks and troops began rolling into these areas.

22 February 2022
Christian Adams
Evening Standard

28 February 2022
Christian Adams
Evening Standard

On 24 February, the Russian invasion of Ukraine commenced. It opened with air and missile attacks on Ukrainian military facilities, before troops and tanks rolled across the borders from the north, east and south. In his previous professional life as an actor, Ukrainian President Volodymyr Zelensky had been the voice of much-loved children's character Paddington Bear, in the Ukrainian-dubbed versions of the films *Paddington* (2014) and *Paddington 2* (2017). Now, Zelensky was pitted against the 'Russian bear' – the traditional depiction of sprawling Russia ever since the old imperial days.

Television screens and social media were full of images of burning buildings following the Russian invasion of Ukraine. Reports also bore witness to the hundreds of thousands of Ukrainians rushing west, to escape the war. In the face of the crisis, EU countries scrambled to introduce a three-year visa waiver for Ukrainians fleeing the conflict. Kevin Foster, a minister working for Priti Patel in the Home Office, was asked on Twitter about the UK's response. His reply highlighted the existing 'seasonal work scheme' for any Ukrainians without family already in the UK. Such was the outcry that the tweet was deleted.

28 February 2022
Morten Morland
The Times

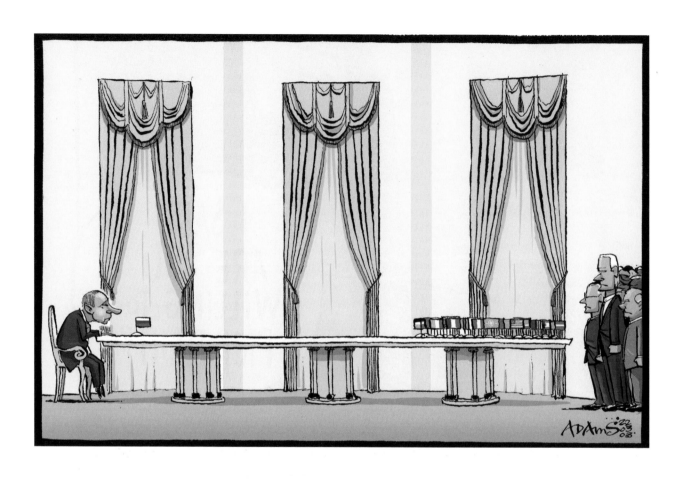

Russia's diplomatic isolation was amply demonstrated by the outcome of a rare 'Special Session' of the UN General Assembly. A resolution demanding that Russia 'immediately, completely and unconditionally withdraw all of its military forces from the territory of Ukraine' was supported by 141 countries. A mere four countries supported Russia: Belarus, North Korea, Eritrea and Syria. (China, Cuba and 33 others abstained.) While Putin had made visiting Western leaders sit at the other end of his enormous table, now it was most of the world putting distance between themselves and Russia.

2 March 2022
Christian Adams
Evening Standard

The day after the invasion of Ukraine began and Kyiv came under attack, the Ukrainian Ministry of Defence went on social media to urge citizens to 'make Molotov cocktails' in readiness to help repel the invaders. The Ukrainian government explained that 'during the Soviet–Finnish War in 1939, the Finnish army fought tanks' with these homemade bombs, manufactured from bottles filled with flammable liquid. The name derives from Stalin's foreign minister, Vyacheslav Molotov, who was understandably not popular with the Finns.

2 March 2022
Brian Adcock
Independent

As the British government threatened sanctions against leading businesspeople associated with Putin, Roman Abramovich, the billionaire owner of Chelsea FC, announced that he was selling the club and would not demand repayment for his £1.5 billion of loans to Chelsea. Moreover, he promised that proceeds from the sale would go into a foundation 'for the benefit of all victims of the war in Ukraine'. Nevertheless, on 10 March Abramovich was among seven people sanctioned by the UK government, which described him as a 'pro-Kremlin oligarch'. Chelsea FC and other of his UK assets were frozen.

3 March 2022
Christian Adams
Evening Standard

Although the Winter Olympic Games were over by the time the Ukraine War began, they were to be followed by the Paralympic Games on 4 March. Two days before, the International Paralympic Committee declared that athletes from Russia (and Russia's ally Belarus) would be allowed to take part, albeit under a neutral flag. There was immediate uproar and threats of a boycott by other countries. In less than 24 hours, the committee executed a U-turn and banned 83 Russian and Belarusian sportspeople. The committee's president acknowledged that the 'rapidly escalating situation' had put them in a 'unique and impossible position'.

3 March 2022
Steven Camley
Herald Scotland

On 4 March, Vladimir Putin signed new measures into law cracking down on free speech. As the cartoonist put it, the effect was to threaten 'citizens and journalists spreading "false information" with 15 years in prison'. It became illegal to use the words 'war' or 'invasion' about Ukraine, since the Kremlin continued to insist it was a 'special military operation'. Criticism of the armed forces and their deployment was banned, as was showing support for sanctions against Russia. As the cartoonist summarised it, 'Putin's propaganda machines spew out Putinspeak. Who could not be reminded of Orwell?'

6 March 2022
Andy Davey
Daily Telegraph

By early March, Russian forces were besieging the city of Mariupol in the Donetsk region of south-eastern Ukraine. Although many civilians had fled the city, an estimated 200,000 were still trapped there, with food, water and medicine supplies running low. The Red Cross attempted to coordinate evacuation corridors under temporary ceasefires, but the shelling continued. On 6 March, the Red Cross reported that 'amid devastating scenes of human suffering' their second attempt at evacuation had once again 'come to a halt' due to continued Russian shelling. The Kremlin said attacks would only stop 'if Kyiv ceases hostilities and fulfils the well-known demands of Russia'.

7 March 2022
Patrick Blower
Daily Telegraph

BREAKING.....Brave Russian troops target next generation of Neo-nazis.   BREAKING.....Brave Ru

10 March 2022
Steven Camley
Herald Scotland

On 9 March, during another attempted ceasefire in Mariupol, a Russian airstrike hit a maternity hospital, resulting in a reported 17 injuries and several deaths. The attack incurred worldwide condemnation, and Ukrainian President Volodymyr Zelensky described the attack as the 'ultimate evidence of genocide' on the part of Russian forces. Russian diplomats and state media hit back, claiming the building was a headquarters for the Azov Regiment, and was legitimately targeted to 'deNazify' Ukraine. A month later, the Organization for Security and Co-operation in Europe (OSCE) classified the hospital attack as a war crime.

The Ukraine War was witnessing a race to the exit door from international companies operating in Russia. The Yale School of Management estimated that by the second week of March around 300 companies were involved in this exodus. Early on, Mastercard and Visa announced they would not process Russian payments. Then, big names in manufacturing and retail joined the boycott, and prominent brands in the world of food and drink announced suspension of operations or supply in Russia, including Coca-Cola, Pepsi, McDonald's and Starbucks.

10 March 2022
Patrick Blower
Daily Telegraph

The UK government's response to the Ukrainian refugee crisis continued to attract criticism – for its cumbersome visa bureaucracy, for the modest numbers arriving, and for failing to match the more generous offer from EU countries. On 14 March, Michael Gove announced the 'Homes for Ukraine' scheme, whereby anyone offering to take in a Ukrainian family would receive a monthly sponsorship of £350. The cartoon alludes to the 1970s hotel-based sitcom *Fawlty Towers*, featuring the irascible Basil Fawlty, his hectoring wife Sybil, and their frequently baffled Spanish employee Manuel, whose catchphrase was 'Que?'

14 March 2022
Brian Adcock
Independent

On 16 March, Boris Johnson visited Saudi Arabia and the United Arab Emirates. Having promised to end imports of oil from Russia by the end of 2022, the prime minister looked first to the Middle East to make up the shortfall – the 8 per cent of UK oil currently coming from Russia – and to help wean the West off Russian energy dependence. However, the previous week the Saudi human rights record again made headlines after the regime executed 81 men in a single day. Johnson promised to raise the issue of human rights, but Keir Starmer accused him of going 'cap in hand from dictator to dictator'.

15 March 2022
Ben Jennings
Guardian

While in Saudi Arabia, Boris Johnson announced himself 'thrilled' at the release of the UK-Iranian dual national Nazanin Zaghari-Ratcliffe, after her highly controversial six-year detention in Iran. But Johnson continued to be dogged by references to his 2017 gaffe, when, as foreign secretary, he had publicly referred to her as 'simply teaching people journalism'. His words were eagerly embraced by the Iranian regime to bolster its allegation that she was engaged in spying and propaganda. Johnson had to apologise in Parliament. Two months after her release, Zaghari-Ratcliffe apparently told the prime minister that his ill-chosen words had exerted a 'lasting impact'.

17 March 2022
Dave Brown
Independent

On 17 March, Lia Thomas's victory in the 500-yard swimming final of the US National Collegiate Athletic Association championship made international news. She was the first transgender woman to win such a prestigious prize. Her victory, though, fuelled the debate about the rules regarding gender identity and sport, with critics (ranging from sportswomen to Boris Johnson) claiming that transgender women had an unfair physical advantage and should be excluded from women's competitions. Meanwhile, in March the transgender cyclist Emily Bridges was forbidden from entering high-level women's competition.

21 March
Steve Bright
Sun

Boris Johnson prompted a clamour of disapproval in his speech to the Conservative spring conference on 19 March. He spoke of Ukraine's instinct 'to choose freedom' instead of tyranny and offered, as a comparison, the vote for Brexit – adding that those voters were not 'remotely hostile to foreigners'. Conservative grandee Lord Heseltine called Johnson's words a 'cynical exploitation of the incredible bravery of the Ukrainian people'. Donald Tusk, formerly president of the European Council, said: 'Boris, your words offend Ukrainians, the British and common sense.' Albrecht Dürer's woodcut of 1498 showed the Four Horsemen of the Apocalypse: Death, Famine, War and Plague.

On 7 March, P&O Ferries announced that nearly 800 employees had been made redundant, most via a mass video-call. Within days, the RMT union claimed that some Indian workers brought in to provide a replacement workforce were being paid just £1.80 per hour. P&O's chief executive later admitted that replacement workers were being paid less than the national minimum wage because foreign-registered vessels and international routes lay outside the scope of UK legislation. Meanwhile, the Insolvency Service 'commenced formal criminal and civil investigations' into the dismissals.

22 March 2022
Steven Camley
Herald Scotland

MICRO TINY MINI BUDGET...

?!

LIVING STANDARDS PLUMMET

DAVID SIMONDS 24.3.22

The Labour Party continued to argue for a windfall tax on gas and oil companies, to provide for large government intervention against the rising cost of living. These companies were accruing massive profits from the high prices of the commodities they produced. Rishi Sunak had promised that his spring statement (23 March) would support 'hard-pressed' families through a 'stronger, more secure economy'. However, the Office for Budget Responsibility estimated that the measures he announced – like a temporary cut in fuel duty and raising the threshold for paying National Insurance – would only soften the effect of already announced tax increases by about one-quarter.

24 March 2022
David Simonds
Evening Standard

On 26 March, President Biden appeared to depart from the prepared text of a speech he was giving in Warsaw, as he exclaimed: 'For God's sake, this man cannot remain in power!' This reference to Vladimir Putin immediately rang alarm bells and, as the *Sun* put it, White House officials 'frantically backtracked' and insisted that the president was not actually announcing a policy of regime change. Two days later, the 94th Academy Awards – the Oscars – took place in Los Angeles. That same day, Biden made 'no apologies' for his earlier words, asserting that they simply expressed his 'moral outrage'.

28 March 2022
Patrick Blower
Daily Telegraph

1 April 2022
Andy Davey
Daily Telegraph

When the Russian defence minister announced in March that Russia would henceforth focus on the Donbas region in the Ukraine War, the news was taken by much of the world as an admission of military failure. At the same time, Western intelligence claimed that Putin's fearful subordinates were keeping him in the dark about the true military situation. As the cartoonist put it, 'Vladimir Putin became increasingly deranged in his TV messages, obviously concealing tremendous rage at the lack of glorious military success. His advisers were rumoured to be scared to tell him the truth. It all begins to look like the Berlin bunker.'

STUCK

RUSSIA UKRAINE

PEACE TALKS

Despite the ferocity of airstrikes and military clashes in Ukraine, tentative peace talks were under way in Istanbul. Ukraine proposed that it could adopt a neutral, non-nuclear status if Russia guaranteed its sovereignty and security, while Russian offered to 'drastically reduce' military operations in western and northern Ukraine. In some circles, Ukraine had been compared to a porcupine, able to inflict pain on the bigger Russian bear. Boris Johnson said that the G7 should support Ukraine until 'the quills of the porcupine have become so stiff' that the country is 'ever after indigestible to Putin'.

1 April 2022
Kevin Kallaugher
Economist

With news that the Metropolitan Police were imposing 20 fixed penalty notices on participants at Downing Street parties, Keir Starmer took aim at Boris Johnson during Prime Minister's Questions on 30 March. Describing the fines as evidence of 'widespread criminality', he accused Johnson of 'taking the British public for fools' and asked: 'Why is he still here?' In the wake of the 54-per-cent rise in the energy price cap, Starmer also attacked Rishi Sunak's spring statement for increasing tax burdens. A few days later, the chancellor flew off for the Easter recess to the £5-million ocean-view penthouse his wife owns in Santa Monica, California.

3 April 2022
Chris Riddell
Observer

The withdrawal of Russian forces from around Kyiv left evidence not only of intense fire-fights, but also horrifying scenes suggesting widescale atrocities against civilians. As officials and journalists entered the city of Bucha, they found clusters of victims who had been executed. Surviving citizens were able to identify dead family members, neighbours and friends, and often to relate the manner of their deaths. There were also reports of hostage-taking, rape and looting by Russian troops. The UK and other countries offered help with evidence-gathering for war crimes prosecutions by the International Criminal Court, while President Zelensky called the killings in Bucha 'genocide'.

4 April 2022
Brian Adcock
Independent

On 4 April, Nadine Dorries posted tweets confirming that the government would try to sell off Channel 4, even though the public-service broadcaster was funded by advertising. She therefore rejected the broadcaster's own 20-year plan for its future in favour of something that, she asserted, could compete with 'streaming giants like Netflix and Amazon'. Later, in the *Mail on Sunday*, she dismissed critics as members of the 'Leftie luvvie lunch mob', whose 'overblown reaction' reflected 'the same people who snobbishly decried my appointment'. The popular Channel 4 reality show *Gogglebox* depicts the reactions of members of the public as they watch TV.

5 April 2022
Christian Adams
Evening Standard

DAVID SIMONDS 7.4.22

Despite European sanctions against Russia, varying levels of dependence on Russian energy at a time of skyrocketing prices seemed to put EU countries in the ugly position of bankrolling Putin's war effort. Josep Borrell, the EU's foreign policy chief, said that though the EU had pledged €1 billion to Ukraine in 'arms and weapons', EU member states were paying that amount daily for Russian energy. On 6 April, MEPs voted overwhelmingly for an 'immediate, full embargo' on those supplies. (The 'z' symbol had been adopted in Russian patriotic propaganda to connote pro-war support.)

7 April 2022
David Simonds
Evening Standard

It was revealed that the chancellor's wealthy wife, Akshata Murty, had for years benefitted from 'non-domicile' status to protect her foreign-earned income from almost all UK income tax. Keir Starmer called the revelation 'breathtaking hypocrisy' as Rishi Sunak 'imposed tax rise after tax rise' on UK working people. (A defensive Sunak invoked the recent Academy Awards, during which actor Will Smith had defended his wife from the host's humour with the injunction to 'Keep my wife's name out of your fucking mouth!') A day later, Murty backtracked and declared she would voluntarily pay UK tax on worldwide earnings henceforth.

8 April 2022
Steven Camley
Herald Scotland

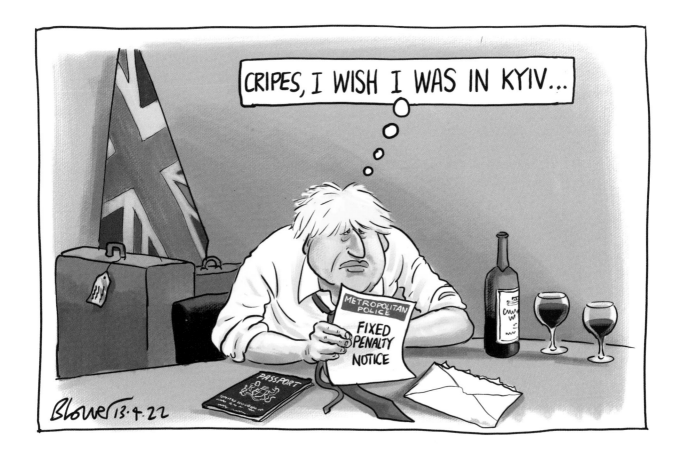

Returning from a surprise visit to Kyiv, during which he was lionised by Ukrainian politicians, Boris Johnson received a fixed penalty notice from the Metropolitan Police – and many calls for his resignation. Carrie Johnson and Rishi Sunak were also fined for the same breach of lockdown rules at the prime minister's 'birthday party' on 19 June 2020. Declaring 'I fully respect' the decision, Johnson nevertheless insisted 'it did not occur to me' that rules were being broken at the event 'lasting less than 10 minutes'. The fine meant he had broken the law, although fixed penalty notices do not generate a criminal record.

13 April 2022
Patrick Blower
Daily Telegraph

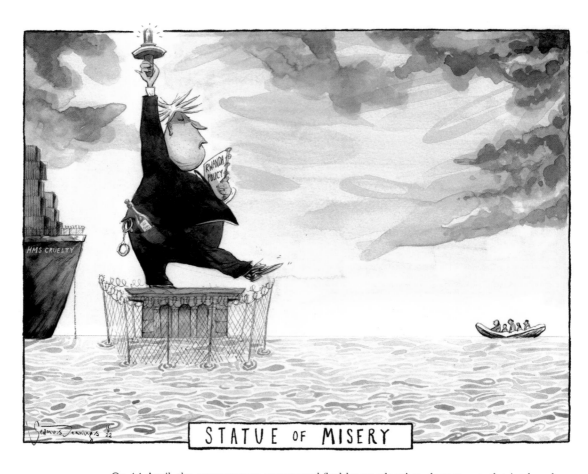

STATUE OF MISERY

16 April 2022
Seamus Jennings
The Times

On 14 April, the government announced 'bold new plans' to deport unauthorised asylum seekers. In this 'partnership' scheme, the deportees would have their 'asylum claim processed' in Rwanda, where those who passed the test would be 'supported to build a new and prosperous life'. Among the many condemning the scheme, the UN Refugee Agency (UNHCR) called it a breach of international law. It seemed far from the spirit of the Statue of Liberty, whose inscribed poem begins: 'Give me your tired, your poor, your huddled masses yearning to breathe free.'

On 14 April, Russian media reported that the flagship of its Black Sea Fleet, *Moskva*, had sunk in 'stormy seas' after an explosion rocked the ship's ammunition stores. By contrast, Ukraine declared that it had targeted the vessel with two of its land-based Neptune missiles. (Later reports suggested that US intelligence had given the Ukrainian military details of the ship's location.) While most of the ship's crew were rescued, there appeared to be at least 28 dead and missing, including the captain. Whatever the truth of the *Moskva*'s demise, it was an embarrassing Russian loss.

16 April 2022
Steven Camley
Herald Scotland

20 April 2022
Christian Adams
Evening Standard

In the week after taking tea with the Queen, Prince Harry told a US television network that he was keen to see her 'protected', with the 'right people around her', prompting questions about whom or what she needed protecting from. While he hoped to attend the monarch's Platinum Jubilee, he alluded to ongoing wrangles over 'security issues and everything else'. The day before, Conservative MP and ex-whip Mark Harper made public his letter of no-confidence in 'a prime minister who broke the laws', whom he thought 'no longer worthy of the great office he holds'. Boris Johnson had just addressed Parliament following his Partygate fine.

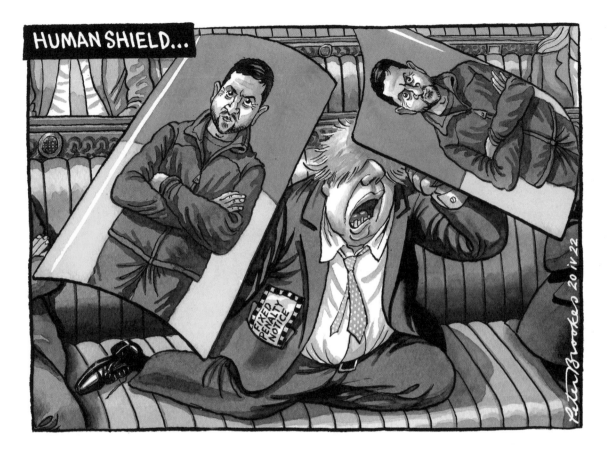

Boris Johnson faced a backlash for using the plight of Ukrainians to distract from his own woes as he apologised for breaking Covid-19 lockdown rules. The prime minister told Parliament that it was 'because I know so many people are angry and disappointed' that he felt 'a greater sense of obligation' to respond to 'Putin's barbaric onslaught'. Keir Starmer responded that it was 'offensive' that Johnson was using Ukraine as a 'shield' to deflect from the fixed penalty notices. According to the cartoonist, '[Johnson] made a great play of supporting Ukraine, while actually of course he was using it to hide from everything that was going wrong at home . . . I was very pleased to find a way of capturing that in this cartoon.'

20 April 2022
Peter Brookes
The Times

THE NIGHTMARE

Davey after Henry Fuseli

The cartoon reinterprets Henry Fuseli's 1781 gothic-horror visualisation of a sleeping woman's dream in the light of the 2022 French presidential election. As the cartoonist explained: 'Thinking about Emmanuel Macron v. Marine Le Pen in the French presidential run-off, the word "nightmare" must have drifted into my head, and almost instantly I had Henry Fuseli's much-admired and much-abused prefiguring of Freud. Fuseli's horrific incubus is replaced by a horrific little devil, Le Pen, on the supine body of France (Marianne). Macron adopts the role of the weird-looking horse.' The figure of Marianne is the post-revolutionary personification of France.

23 April 2022
Andy Davey
Jewish Chronicle

On 20 April, Russia test-launched its new intercontinental ballistic missile, the Satan II, after which Valdimir Putin declared that 'it would make those who threaten our country think twice.' A presenter on Russian state TV then boasted that nuclear missiles (if launched from Kaliningrad) could destroy Paris, Berlin and London in 200 seconds. At the end of the classic gangster film *White Heat* (1949), the deranged protagonist, played by James Cagney, dies atop a spherical exploding gas-tank after shouting 'Made it Ma! Top of the world!' ('Uncle Joe' was the nickname for Stalin propagated during the Second World War, although President Biden has also been referred to this way.)

27 April 2022
Dave Brown
Independent

News emerged that two female Conservative MPs had complained about a male colleague watching pornography on his smartphone in Parliament, including inside the Commons chamber. The media were rife with speculation as to the identity of the offender. The cartoonist said: 'I chose Jacob Rees-Mogg [as the disciplinarian], as he had been tasked with the whereabouts of MPs in Parliament ... The *Guardian* were very keen that the other characters in the cartoon remain anonymous.' Rees-Mogg had recently taken to leaving notes on the desks of MPs who were working from home, saying he looked forward to seeing them 'in the office very soon'.

29 April 2022
Peter Songi
Guardian

On 25 April, the board of Twitter accepted the offer of $44 billion from the platform's biggest shareholder, Elon Musk, to take control of the company. Musk had presented himself as a 'free speech absolutist', which led to an expectation that he would relax Twitter's current controls. These had, for example, seen Donald Trump's account 'permanently' suspended on 8 January 2021, following the Capitol Hill rioting. The cartoon parodies the film *Braveheart* (1995). I'm aware that this cartoon was created by an Irish cartoonist for an Irish publication and so is at odds with the title of this book, but as it offers such an interesting visual commentary on an important event, I hope Irish readers will forgive the inclusion.

30 April 2022
Harry Burton
Irish Examiner

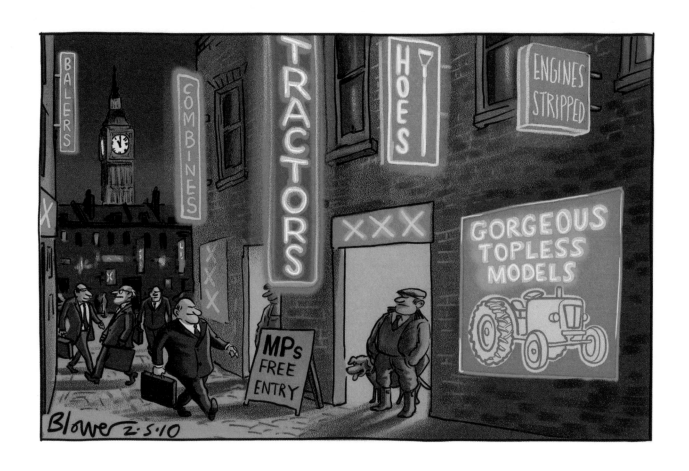

Blower 2·5·10

2 May 2022
Patrick Blower
Daily Telegraph

By 29 April, Neil Parish was revealed as the MP who had been observed watching porn in Parliament. His initial refusal to stand down as an MP swiftly converted into his resignation the next day. In an interview with BBC South West, he explained that 'funnily enough, it was tractors I was looking at' when he chanced upon a similarly named porn website. However, he admitted that his 'biggest crime' – his 'moment of madness' – was to go into the site deliberately on a second occasion. The media quickly dubbed him 'tractor porn MP'.

Environment Secretary George Eustice courted controversy after suggesting that people switching to 'value brands' could 'contain and manage their household budget' in the face of sharply rising food prices. Liberal Democrat spokesperson Wendy Chamberlain called the comments 'patronising advice from a clueless minister'. Consumer champion Martin Lewis though it was 'bullshit' to think that low earners did not already choose 'value brands' and said the challenges were much bigger than that. Poverty campaigner Jack Monroe remarked that 'a man who claims around 200 grand in personal expenses' was in 'absolutely no position to lecture anyone about the price of biscuits'.

5 May 2022
Steven Camley
Herald Scotland

Two days before local elections, Boris Johnson was interviewed on *Good Morning Britain* amid predictions of big Conservative losses. Host Susanna Reid sought his views on the case of 77-year-old Elsie who faced an increase in her energy bills from £17 to £85 per month. Elsie was, Reid explained, resorting to 'eating one meal a day', buying reduced-price food that had reached its sell-by date, and using her Freedom bus pass 'to stay on buses all day to avoid using energy at home'. When Johnson boasted that 'the Freedom bus pass was something I actually introduced,' his tone-deafness prompted Reid to exclaim: 'So, Elsie should be grateful to you for her bus pass?!'

5 May 2022
Dave Brown
Independent

On 5 May, the 30 countries of NATO signed an 'accession protocol', paving the way for Sweden and Finland to take part in NATO meetings in advance of fully joining the alliance. For both countries this was a radical step: Sweden had a long history of neutrality, including throughout both world wars, while Finland's neutrality had been born of a delicate balancing act between Russia and the west, nurtured after conflicts with Russia in the 20th century. The catalyst for both countries' pivot was Putin's naked aggression in invading Ukraine.

6 May 2022
Steve Bell
Guardian

On 5 May, *Politico* published a rare, leaked document from the US Supreme Court. It was a draft majority opinion, written by Justice Samuel Alito, which overturned two landmark rulings (*Roe v. Wade* of 1973 and *Planned Parenthood v. Casey* of 1992) and therefore removed the constitutional right to abortion. Decisions over abortion laws would now revert to individual states, and Republican state governments opposed to abortion quickly enacted 'trigger laws' to ban abortion when the court's ruling became official. Grant Wood's celebrated painting *American Gothic* (1930) depicted a Midwestern farmer and his daughter outside their 'carpenter gothic'-style farmhouse. I'm aware that this cartoon was created by an Irish cartoonist for an Irish publication and so is at odds with the title of this book, but as it offers such an interesting visual commentary on an important event, I hope Irish readers will forgive the inclusion.

7 May 2022
Harry Burton
Irish Examiner

Some relief came for Boris Johnson when the media renewed their interest in a potential example of lockdown rule-breaking by Labour: 'Beergate'. On 6 May 2022, Durham Constabulary agreed to investigate the events of 30 April 2021, in which Keir Starmer had been caught on video holding a beer while others ate curry in the Durham office of MP Mary Foy, shortly before the Hartlepool by-election. Starmer later implied that ordering food was a spontaneous decision, but a leaked memo suggested that a casual dinner slot was planned. On 9 May, Starmer and his deputy, Angela Rayner, agreed that they would resign if they were issued with fixed penalty notices.

9 May 2022
Steve Bright
Sun

Following the accession protocols of 5 May, it was now up to Sweden and Finland's politicians to apply formally to join NATO. In Finland (whose border with Russia stretches for more than 800 miles) the president and prime minister called for membership 'without delay' – and opinion polls suggested that 75 per cent of Finns agreed with them. In Sweden, the ruling Social Democrats backed NATO membership, and polls showed steadily rising support among Swedes, reaching 60 per cent in May. Putin's press chief, Dmitry Peskov, warned darkly of 'military-technical' responses if Finland joined, but to no avail. On 18 May, Sweden and Finland put in simultaneous NATO applications.

13 May 2022
Kevin Kallaugher
Economist

A letter leaked to *ITV News* confirmed that Boris Johnson and senior ministers wanted to save money by culling 91,000 staff from the civil service payroll, representing a fifth of the workforce. According to the cartoonist, 'Jacob Rees-Mogg wanted to get back to 2016 levels of staffing before Brexit and the pandemic, and called it "getting back to normal". The FDA civil service union was, meanwhile, in "open revolt", calling for permanent flexible working arrangements in "neutral" locations, saying work should no longer be considered a "place". The Moggster seemed to agree – at least for 91,000 of them.'

14 May 2022
Andy Davey
Daily Telegraph

The UK's Sam Ryder came second in the 66th Eurovision Song Contest after a huge wave of audience support for Ukraine's winning entry. Ukraine's song – the folk-rap fusion 'Stefania', performed by Kalush Orchestra – was ostensibly about a band-member's mother, but transformed into a patriotic anthem. A day after the invasion of Ukraine, the European Broadcasting Union, which administers Eurovision, had banned Russia from taking part. On the day of the competition in host country Italy, police blocked several Russian-based cyber-attacks on the broadcasting networks.

16 May 2022
Morten Morland
The Times

On 17 May, Foreign Secretary Liz Truss made clear the government's intention to table legislation that would scrap parts of the Northern Ireland Protocol agreed with the EU. While claiming the move was consistent with international law, her statement fuelled criticism from European leaders and the EU president, Ursula von der Leyen. Her vice-president, Maroš Šefčovič, promised an EU response 'with all measures at its disposal' if the UK took this course. Meanwhile, EU member states, under pressure to impose an energy embargo on Russia, were struggling to agree how and when to wean themselves off reliance on Russian gas and oil.

18 May 2022
Patrick Blower
Daily Telegraph

On 19 May, the Metropolitan Police announced the closure of Operation Hillman examining the 'alleged breaches of Covid regulations' at Downing Street and Whitehall. The final tally of fixed penalty notice referrals was 126, for eight events investigated over 11 months. It turned out that 28 people were fined between two and five times – though names were not released. Boris Johnson had escaped with just the one fine, for his birthday event, but that did not prevent Labour from renewing calls for his resignation and attacking what Angela Rayner called 'industrial-scale rule-breaking'.

20 May 2022
David Simonds
Evening Standard

The news of yet another mass school shooting in the United States led to heartbreak, protests and recriminations over police responses, yet offered little prospect of politicians agreeing fundamental reform to the country's gun laws. On 24 May, 18-year-old Salvador Ramos used an assault weapon to murder 19 children and two teachers at Robb Elementary School in Uvalde, Texas. Police did not engage him for more than an hour and a quarter before a tactical unit shot him dead. That evening, in an emotional appeal, President Biden lamented the lives lost before asking: 'When in God's name are we going to stand up to the gun lobby?'

25 May 2022
David Simonds
Evening Standard

When ITV News released new pictures of Downing Street gatherings under lockdown restrictions, most of the people depicted in them were pixelated and unidentifiable. Not so Boris Johnson, clearly seen raising a glass to his departing director of communications, Lee Cain, on 13 November 2020, while near him on tables lay party snacks and bottles of wine and gin. His assurances to the House of Commons that no rules had been broken – or that he had been unaware of rules being breached – seemed increasingly to strain credulity, including among his own MPs.

25 May 2022
Dave Brown
Independent

On 24 May, the long-delayed Elizabeth Line – colloquially 'Crossrail' – finally opened for its inaugural run across central London. The public flocked to try out the purple-liveried trains and the state-of-the-art stations. Meanwhile, Boris Johnson faced resurgent backbench discontent, as MPs' inboxes were filling again with constituents' ire over Partygate following the latest pictures. One persistent critic, Sir Roger Gale, who believed Johnson had misled the Commons, tweeted: 'This is a resignation issue.' Another complained anonymously that 'We're all getting tired of making excuses for Boris.'

25 May 2022
Patrick Blower
Daily Telegraph

With the Metropolitan Police investigation of Partygate over, Sue Gray's full report on the gatherings was published on 25 May. Boris Johnson's subsequent statement to the House of Commons acknowledged his own fixed penalty fine at a 'short lunchtime' event but characterised his presence at staff leaving parties as 'one of the essential duties of leadership'. He distanced himself from what happened after he left those events, describing himself as 'appalled by some of the behaviour' Gray described. He pronounced himself 'humbled', before lauding the achievements of his government.

26 May 2022
Steven Camley
Herald Scotland

The day after the publication of Sue Gray's report, Chancellor Rishi Sunak splashed the cash in the face of the rising cost of living and soaring bills. He announced extra borrowing and a 25 per cent windfall tax on the huge profits of oil and gas companies – a policy that Labour had been demanding. This income was meant to bankroll £15 billion of payments, including £400 towards every household energy bill, with additional payments for older pensioners and those on means-tested benefits. He claimed that the poorest families would therefore receive at least £1,200 and would 'know the government is standing by them'.

27 May 2022
Steve Bell
Guardian

1 June 2022
Patrick Blower
Daily Telegraph

As the summer half-term break approached, including an extended holiday weekend for the Queen's Platinum Jubilee, many families were hoping to board flights to foreign destinations. But British airports witnessed scenes of chaos as airlines – too understaffed to cope with surging demand after Covid-19 restrictions ended – were overwhelmed. By the start of June, as airports filled with long queues and angry customers, EasyJet, British Airways and TUI had announced hundreds of flight cancellations. While some customers could not get away, others found themselves stranded abroad, awaiting rescheduled flights.

According to the cartoonist, 'Russia's war in Ukraine entered its 100th day. NATO warned it had become a "war of attrition". [Ukrainian President] Zelensky said Moscow's forces were in control of 20 per cent of Ukrainian territory, some of which constituted the "Ukrainian breadbasket" which fed the world.' Russia was accused of stealing grain from occupied territory and using its blockade of the Black Sea to cripple Ukraine's hugely significant wheat exports. The *Guardian* estimated that Ukrainian grain fed 400 million people, many of them in the developing world. Now, the United Nations warned that millions could die from starvation, while Putin dangled the possibility of a safe corridor in return for the West rowing back on sanctions against Russia.

4 June 2022
Andy Davey
Daily Telegraph

The celebrations for the Queen's Platinum Jubilee included, on 4 June, a 'Platinum Party' – a live musical extravaganza performed in front of Buckingham Palace. It was introduced by a short film sketch, in which Paddington Bear took tea with the Queen and offered his own congratulations: 'Happy Jubilee Ma'am, and thank you, for everything.' Just a few days before, an effusive Keir Starmer, writing in the *Daily Telegraph*, had lauded the Queen's 'commitment to duty and passion for furthering our country'. Under Jeremy Corbyn, the Labour party had been accused of lukewarm support for the monarchy, a perception some pollsters linked to declining Labour backing.

6 June 2022
Steve Bright
Sun

STUBBORN STAINS...

On 6 June, Boris Johnson narrowly survived a vote of confidence in his leadership, but no less than 148 Conservative MPs – representing 41 per cent of the parliamentary party – refused to support him. His opponents and critics, and much of the media, dwelt on the loss of authority that the revolt suggested. By contrast, Johnson himself was bullish, claiming a 'good, positive, conclusive' result and that the government could now 'draw a line' under Partygate. Sue Gray's report into Partygate had recounted how cleaners had found wine stains besmirching a wall at Number 10 after one event.

8 June 2022
Dave Brown
Independent

As the cost of refuelling a car soared to more than £100 for a 'typical' 55-litre tank (according to data analysts Experian Catalist), critics rounded on Rishi Sunak and the Treasury. The overall tax take from fuel duty and associated VAT had risen, despite a 5-pence fuel-duty cut in March. By 10 June, Conservative backbencher Sir John Redwood was tweeting that 'the chancellor needs to limit the amount he plunders from us at the pumps.' On 13 June, the government ordered the Competition and Markets Authority to investigate whether retailers were actually passing on the fuel-duty cut to consumers.

9 June 2022
Christian Adams
Evening Standard

Despite the efforts of super-loyalist Nadine Dorries to dismiss Boris Johnson's opponents, and despite the prime minister's own efforts to change the subject in a speech about extending home ownership, the chorus of disapproval remained stubborn. In the words of the cartoonist, 'Nadine Dorries demonstrated a desperate loyalty to a washed-up Boris, out of ideas, trying to rehash a failed Margaret Thatcher right-to-buy policy, in an attempt to distract us from Partygate. The prime minister was even booed at by royalists at the Queen's Platinum Jubilee. Jeremy Hunt is in the foreground, revving up for a leadership contest.'

10 June 2022
Henny Beaumont
Guardian

A government policy paper (13 June) entitled 'Food Strategy for England' promised much: a 'sustainable, nature-positive, affordable food system' in a 'prosperous agri-food and sea-food sector' filled with 'high-quality jobs around the country'. Absent, though, was a key health-driven tax on processed food and catering, as recommended by restaurateur Henry Dimbleby's independent review of the national food strategy in 2021. In the cartoonist's words, 'As food prices soared, Boris Johnson U-turned on his food strategy and rejected calls for a tax on salt and sugar.' Johnson had incurred a fixed penalty notice for his lockdown birthday party, famously featuring a cake.

13 June 2022
Nicola Jennings
Guardian

THE MORAL WAY TO FILL ONE-WAY FLIGHTS OUT OF HERE...

15 VI 22

Peter Brookes

A last-minute legal intervention scuppered the maiden flight of asylum seekers to Rwanda for processing and possible settlement there. The plane was supposed to have departed in May with around 130 asylum seekers, but by mid-June its occupants had shrunk to seven. Then, on 13 June, the European Court of Human Rights granted an 'urgent interim measure' in respect of one deportee, an Iraqi national, giving him a three-week reprieve pending 'the final domestic decision' in the judicial review regarding his case. Plenty of opposition to the Rwanda scheme had questioned its morality, and the cartoonist imagines a planeload of government ministers on a one-way ticket.

15 June 2022
Peter Brookes
The Times

On 16 June, Lord Geidt became the second of Boris Johnson's ethics advisers – formally, the 'Independent Adviser on Ministers' Interests' – to resign. He revealed that he 'could not be a party to advising on any potential law-breaking' after he had been asked to advise on an 'odious' breach of the ministerial code. Following Geidt's resignation, Number 10 suggested that the role of ethics adviser might be scrapped altogether. Lord Evans, chair of the Committee of Standards on Public Life, warned that axing the post would 'further damage public perceptions of standards'. Here, the cartoonist imagines which applicants might suit Johnson's impatience with the rules.

18 June 2022
Ben Jennings
Guardian

THE LONGEVITY TEST

STRIKE

I CAN DO THIS ALL YEAR...

When the largest rail strike in several decades began on 21 June, Mick Lynch, leader of the biggest union involved (the RMT), warned that further strikes were 'extremely likely' if agreement over pay and conditions was not reached with the rail companies and Network Rail. At the same time, the *British Medical Journal* reported a research project suggesting that the ability (or not) of middle-aged and older people to stand on one leg for 10 seconds (or more) predicted the likely risk of death within the next seven years: it was quickly dubbed the 'longevity test'.

22 June 2022
Christian Adams
Evening Standard

24 June 2022
Steve Bell
Guardian

Boris Johnson (as he himself joked) arrived in Rwanda ahead of any intended asylum deportees from the UK. The occasion was a meeting of the Commonwealth heads of government in Rwanda's capital, Kigali. Before flying there, Johnson had expressed the hope that his visit would help combat 'condescending attitudes' towards the country, which he attributed to critics of the asylum-deportation policy. According to media reports, these critics included Prince Charles – representing the Queen at the three-day event – who had supposedly told friends he found the government's scheme 'appalling'.

Conservative knives were sharpened after Boris Johnson suffered several blows to his authority. In the Tiverton and Honiton by-election, the Liberal Democrats overturned a 24,000 majority to turn the true-blue seat yellow. Meanwhile, Labour regained Wakefield to put a dent in the Red Wall of northern seats that had turned Conservative in 2019. The defeats spurred Oliver Dowden, Conservative co-chair, to resign because, as he said, 'somebody must take responsibility'. Former party leader, Michael Howard, responded that it 'may be necessary' for the 1922 Committee to change its rules to allow for another leadership vote. The classic comedy film *Carry on Cleo* (1964) featured the 'infamy' joke, uttered by Kenneth Williams playing Julius Caesar.

25 June 2022
Chris Riddell
Observer

The conservative-leaning US Supreme Court justices delivered a ruling (in the case *Dobbs v. Jackson Women's Health Organization*) that overturned American women's constitutional right to abortion. Almost half of American states were poised to enact new laws (or revive old ones) to ban abortion, in some states even in cases of rape or incest. Protests erupted across the US at the potential consequences of a ruling that diluted women's rights over their own bodies. The wire coat hanger had been a grim symbol of the era of backstreet abortions and dangerous attempts at self-administered terminations, which, in the eyes of some, threatened now to return.

26 June 2022
Nicola Jennings
Guardian

Further questions about the relationship between the Prince of Wales's Charitable Fund and Middle-Eastern donors arose from a *Sunday Times* report on 26 June. It revealed that between 2011 and 2015, the ex-prime minister of Qatar had handed over more than €3 million in cash to the prince, deploying a suitcase and even Fortnum & Mason carrier bags for the purpose. Norman Baker, the veteran anti-monarchist Liberal Democrat, called the episode 'grubby' and tried to get the Metropolitan Police to investigate. Clarence House and Charles's allies insisted the donations were immediately processed in the normal and proper legal way – but it was stressed that such cash donations had been avoided in recent years.

27 June 2022
Steve Bright
Sun

27 June 2022
Patrick Blower
Daily Telegraph

Boris Johnson, still in Kigali, was upbeat about his future, insisting that he would lead Conservatives into the next general election and win it. More than that, he said he was 'thinking actively' about a third prime-ministerial term, which would take him into the 2030s. This imagining of future glories prompted an unnamed former cabinet minister to describe Johnson as 'completely delusional'. The dissident Conservative Andrew Bridgen quipped: 'I'm more than happy for him to stay until 20:30. He can even stay until nine o'clock if he wants, so long as he's gone before Parliament breaks up for summer.'

On 27 June, a Russian missile hit a busy shopping centre in the city of Kremenchuk, in central Ukraine, killing (according to local counts) 20 people, including women and children, and injuring upwards of 50. Initial Russian claims that the event was staged by Ukraine gave way to a second false claim that fire had spread accidentally from a missile targeting an alleged 'arms dump' nearby. G7 leaders, at a summit in Germany, quickly condemned the attack as 'abominable' and declared that 'indiscriminate attacks on innocent civilians constitute a war crime.' They added: 'President Putin and those responsible will be held to account.'

28 June 2022
Christian Adams
Evening Standard

SAME OLD TUNE

Blower 29·6·22

Scottish First Minister Nicola Sturgeon set out her arguments for another referendum on Scottish independence, on the basis that her coalition of the SNP and the Scottish Greens gave her a pro-independence mandate. She also informed Boris Johnson that she was asking the UK Supreme Court to consider whether, in light of Scottish election results, Westminster really had the power to prevent a new referendum. The UK government still insisted that 'now was not the time', while Labour's shadow Scotland secretary called Sturgeon's moves 'a transparent attempt to whip up division'. Opinion polls suggested a narrow majority in Scotland were still opposed to independence.

29 June 2022
Patrick Blower
Daily Telegraph

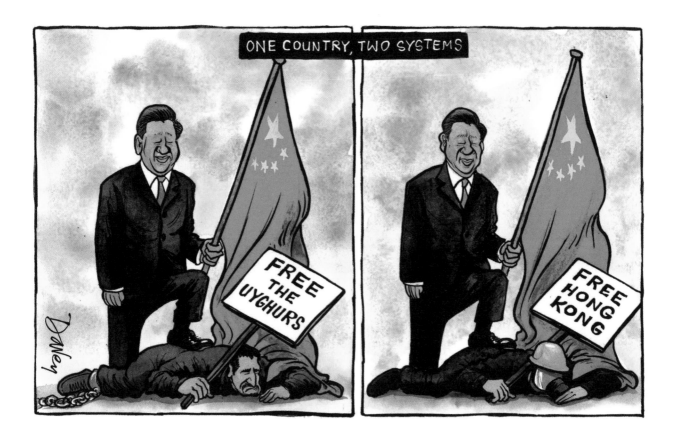

ONE COUNTRY, TWO SYSTEMS

FREE THE UYGHURS

FREE HONG KONG

As explained by the cartoonist, 'On the 25th anniversary of the handover of Hong Kong to Chinese sovereignty, [President] Xi declared that "there is no reason to change" the one country, two systems arrangement under which Hong Kong is governed.' But, his cartoon asked, 'Would these two systems be like the treatment of Uyghurs and of Hong Kong protesters?' Beijing's imposition of a new security law on Hong Kong in 2020 was seen by the West as a blatant attempt to erode democratic rights there, while increasing evidence emerged of the systematic mistreatment of China's Uyghur minority on the mainland.

2 July 2022
Andy Davey
Daily Telegraph

Following a summit in June, NATO countries agreed a 'fundamental shift' in their approach to 'deterrence and defence', all motivated by Putin's invasion of Ukraine. Since the invasion was launched, the number of NATO battlegroups along its eastern border had doubled, from four to eight, and now the defence organisation promised 'to increase the number of high-readiness forces to well over 300,000'. Putin had effectively ushered in what NATO's secretary-general, Jens Stoltenberg, called 'the biggest overhaul of our collective defence and deterrence since the Cold War'.

4 July 2022
Kevin Kallaugher
Economist

On 5 July, Boris Johnson faced the twin resignations of his chancellor and health secretary. The catalyst was Johnson's denial that he had known of 'specific' allegations about sexual misconduct concerning MP Chris Pincher before appointing him as the Conservatives' deputy chief whip. In an unusual move, the former head of the diplomatic service, Lord McDonald, went public to reveal that Johnson's denial could not be true. In resignation letters, Sunak wrote 'we cannot continue like this,' while Javid concluded that the prime minister had 'lost my confidence too'. The 1961 song 'Three Wheels on My Wagon' begins: 'Three wheels on my wagon/ And I'm still rolling along.'

5 July 2022
Steve Bright
Unpublished

THE REMAINER

11 July 2022
Nicola Jennings
Guardian

Rishi Sunak's and Sajid Javid's departures triggered an avalanche of government resignations. Boris Johnson could not even rely on his replacement cabinet, most notably Nadhim Zahawi, who accepted the job of chancellor on 5 July but by 7 July tweeted, 'You must do the right thing and go now.' Johnson announced his resignation, pending a new leader, that day. He spoke of the 'vast mandate' from voters in 2019 and his belief that he was still the man for the job, but he acknowledged that 'no one is remotely indispensable'. Shortly beforehand, education minister Andrea Jenkyns had raised her middle finger at what she called the 'baying mob' outside Downing Street.

Eight of the MPs who declared they were running to replace Boris Johnson were officially nominated by 12 July. Others, such as Sajid Javid and Grant Shapps, had already withdrawn. In an atmosphere of intense rivalry – and amid allegations of dirty tricks – the *Guardian* reported that the candidates' campaign teams were already leaking potentially embarrassing or damaging claims about their competitors to the Labour Party, while also attacking each other on the kind of culture-war and gender-politics issues that were dog-whistles for the party rank and file.

12 July 2022
Steven Camley
Herald Scotland

16 July 2022
Andy Davey
Daily Telegraph

By 16 July, as summer heated up, there were six candidates left in the Conservative leadership race. Rishi Sunak had won the first two rounds of voting among MPs, but a YouGov poll of 879 party members (13 July) suggested that, among the grassroots, Penny Mordaunt was the favourite, with 27 per cent wanting her as leader. In the cartoonist's words, 'she had secured the sunbed.' Mordaunt had briefly been defence secretary before being sacked by Boris Johnson, though she later became a trade minister.

Despite the near-universal acknowledgement that climate change was responsible for the UK experiencing a record-breaking heatwave, only 4 per cent of Conservative Party members placed the achievement of net-zero emissions by 2050 among their top-three policy priorities (according to a YouGov poll conducted for *The Times*). Conservative leadership candidates reflected this lack of interest during television debates. Cabinet member Alok Sharma, who had presided over the COP26 summit, warned he might resign should Boris Johnson's successor renege on the net-zero targets.

19 July 2022
Ben Jennings
Guardian

On 19 July, the Met Office recorded the UK's highest-ever temperature: 40.3 degrees celsius, at Coningsby, in Lincolnshire. That day also witnessed the fourth ballot of Conservative MPs, in which leadership candidates continued to melt away – the latest being Kemi Badenoch, who was eliminated after securing only 59 votes. Badenoch was Boris Johnson's equalities minister until her resignation on 6 July, and she had progressed this far in the contest despite relatively low recognition among the public. Liz Truss appeared to have the most momentum, after picking up an additional 15 votes.

20 July 2022
Dave Brown
Independent

Vladimir Putin arrived in Iran on 19 July, just days after President Biden had concluded a four-day visit to the Middle East. Although pledging, alongside Israel, that Iran would never 'acquire a nuclear weapon', Biden nevertheless held out hope that the internationally brokered 'Iran nuclear deal' could be revived, to keep Iranian nuclear ambitions peaceful. Iran's supreme leader Ayatollah Khamenei, however, showed effusive support for Putin and the invasion of Ukraine, and hostility towards the West and NATO. Russia and Iran signed trade agreements under which, commentators speculated, Iran might sell Russia military drones in exchange for wheat.

20 July 2022
Patrick Blower
Daily Telegraph

So extreme were UK temperatures that the Met Office issued its first-ever heat-related red weather warning because of the potentially life-threatening effects on even the 'fit and healthy'. Wildfires engulfed homes in London, Kent and Yorkshire. The government convened emergency COBRA meetings, but the prime minister was absent from three of them. He was, however, very visible in video footage showing him enjoying a flight in a Typhoon jet from RAF Coningsby. One Twitter user erupted: 'Deadly heat wave, impending gas shortage, soaring food and fuel prices . . . And he's off farting around having a joyride with the RAF?!'

21 July 2022
Guy Venables
Metro

Following the fifth ballot of Conservative MPs (20 July), Penny Mordaunt was eliminated from the race to succeed Boris Johnson, leaving Rishi Sunak and Liz Truss to go head-to-head in September's vote of party members. Jacob Rees-Mogg had come out earlier in support of Truss, giving a press interview in Downing Street alongside Nadine Dorries. The media speculated that the location hinted at tacit endorsement of Truss by Johnson as the 'continuity' candidate. Rees-Mogg stressed Truss's loyalty, saying 'she's stuck by the prime minister.'

21 July 2022
Steven Camley
Herald Scotland

22 July 2022
Andy Davey
Daily Telegraph

As the duel between Rishi Sunak and Liz Truss got under way, Pippa Crerar asked in the *Daily Mirror*: 'What better way to woo the Tory faithful than by positioning themselves as the heir to Margaret Thatcher?' As the cartoonist put it, 'There's no doubt who the candidates think they have to show adoration of: the icon that is Maggie. Sunak says, "I am a Thatcherite, I am running as a Thatcherite," etc, etc. Truss even wore Thatcher's pussybow ensemble to the last debate. It's Maggie all the way.'

With their sights set firmly on winning over the Conservative Party faithful, Truss and Sunak vied with each other to look the toughest on immigration. Sunak hit out at the European Court of Human Rights and insisted that he would 'inject a healthy dose of common sense' into the immigration debate, asking Parliament to set annual caps on refugees accepted into the UK. Truss (like Sunak) reiterated support for the Rwanda deportation policy for migrants and asylum seekers arriving illegally and added that she would pursue similar deals with other countries. Amnesty International described such pledges as 'dreadful'.

25 July 2022
Ben Jennings
Guardian

As the latest industrial action on the railways (27 July) reduced services by four-fifths, Transport Secretary Grant Shapps rejected calls for the government to talk directly with unions and lambasted 'cynically timed' strikes. He warned that he would be prepared to ban strikes 'by different unions in the same workplace within a set period'. Rishi Sunak and Liz Truss both supported strike bans on 'essential services' if they were to be elected leader, with Truss making much of her 'tough line' and defending the public from being 'held ransom by militant unions'. RMT leader Mick Lynch said that any attempts at strike-banning legislation would prompt a general strike.

28 July 2022
Steve Bell
Guardian

MIXED SIGNAL BOX

DON'T STRIKE

STRIKE

SPEED

CAUTION

FULL

RMT PICKET

Blower 28·7·22

There was backlash from union leaders and the left of the Labour Party to Keir Starmer's sacking of his shadow transport minister, Sam Tarry. In June, Starmer had warned his front-bench team to stay away from picket lines and to 'show leadership'. But Tarry joined striking railway staff at Euston Station on 27 July and spoke to the media, asserting his 'solidarity with striking workers'. A Labour spokesman declared that Tarry's media comments meant he was guilty of a 'breach of collective responsibility', while still insisting that the party would 'always stand up for working people fighting for better pay, terms and conditions at work'.

28 July 2022
Patrick Blower
Daily Telegraph

On 26 July, the British public were treated to the fourth television Conservative leadership debate, and the second one featuring just the two final contenders. The latest debate was broadcast by TalkTV in collaboration with the *Sun* newspaper. In the event, it came to a (literally) crashing halt as host Kate McCann fainted and collapsed off-screen, to the on-screen alarm of Liz Truss, who rushed over to her, as did Rishi Sunak. TalkTV issued a statement saying that although McCann was 'fine, the medical advice was that we shouldn't continue with the debate.'

28 July 2022
Dave Brown
Independent

On 31 July, England's women beat old rivals and eight-time champions Germany to win the European Championship 2022. It was the Lionesses' first major trophy – and England's first football trophy since 1966. Over 87,000 fans packed into Wembley Stadium to watch the team make history. According to the cartoonist, 'You'd be hard pressed to find anyone less interested in football than I am. Nevertheless, I was moved by the Lionesses' enthusiasm, energy and skill. They reminded us of what team sports should be about. Consequently, I enjoyed playing around with the national team's logo.'

2 August 2022
Peter Schrank
The Times

THE GREATEST STITCH-VP

SINCE THE BIRTH OF VENVS

© Steve Bell 2022 – AFTER BOTTICELLI + THE BAYEUX TAPESTRY – 2·8·4696 –   Belltoons.co.uk

Boris Johnson joked that his removal as prime minister was 'the greatest stitch-up since the Bayeux Tapestry'. Johnson made the remark at a lavish party to celebrate his wedding which, due to Covid-19, had had limited attendance when it took place in May 2021. Following the celebrations, Liz Truss (who had emerged as the frontrunner to replace Johnson) was asked whether the prime minister should be concentrating on affairs of state. She replied that Johnson had done a 'fantastic job in standing up to Putin, in delivering Brexit and in delivering our Covid vaccine . . . he's entitled to enjoy his wedding day'. The cartoon evokes *The Birth of Venus* (c. 1485) by Sandro Botticelli.

2 August 2022
Steve Bell
Guardian

China launched its largest ever military exercises around Taiwan in response to a visit by Nancy Pelosi, the speaker of the US House of Representatives. Pelosi said that her visit was designed to make it 'unequivocally clear' that the United States would 'not abandon' the island. She also praised Taiwan's commitment to democracy. Shortly after the visit, China deployed ballistic missiles, fighter jets and warships in the Taiwan Strait. China has long viewed Taiwan as part of its territory and has vowed to 'reunify' the island with the Chinese mainland.

5 August 2022
Kevin Kallaugher
Economist

Boris Johnson (who still had a month left in office) and his chancellor, Nadhim Zahawi, both went on holiday as soaring energy prices continued to rock the economy. The Bank of England announced that it was raising interest rates from 1.25 per cent to 1.75 per cent, the single biggest rise since 1995, to control rapid inflation. The Bank forecast that inflation would peak at 13.3 per cent in October, the highest for more than 42 years, and the UK would fall into recession. Former Labour leader Ed Miliband said that the government was 'missing in action' during 'a national emergency', while 'the candidates for the leadership have no substantive ideas about how to help working people.'

7 August 2022
Ben Jennings
Guardian

FBI investigators seized documents from Donald Trump's Mar-a-Lago estate as part of an investigation into whether the former president had removed and destroyed presidential documents. It was believed that Trump had illegally taken 15 boxes of materials with him when he left office. On 8 August, news website Axios published photos, which they claimed showed he had also flushed classified papers down White House toilets while he was president. In 2018, Trump requested that the Guggenheim Museum lend him *Landscape with Snow* (1888) by Vincent Van Gogh for display in the White House. The museum declined but instead offered *America* (2016) by Maurizio Cattelan – a fully functioning, solid gold toilet.

9 August 2022
Christian Adams
Evening Standard

10 August 2022
Dave Brown
Independent

On 9 August it was announced that Olivia Newton-John had died at the age of 73. The actor and musician was catapulted to fame in the 1978 musical sensation, *Grease*. The film gave Newton-John and her co-star, John Travolta, three huge hit singles including 'You're the One That I Want'. Meanwhile, the candidates for the Conservative leadership tore into each other's plans to prevent a cost-of-living crisis. Rishi Sunak accused Liz Truss of a 'major U-turn' after she remarked that she would do 'all that I can' to help households, after previously saying that she favoured tax cuts over 'hand-outs'. Sunak said that he would provide more direct financial support to pensioners and low earners.

According to the cartoonist, 'Rishi Sunak was consistently behind Liz Truss in polls of Tory party members, and the idea that he might catch up was beginning to seem impossible. At the same time, we were entering a heatwave that threatened droughts and a national water shortage. It's often the background details I enjoy the most – such as the parched-brown Tory tree in the background here (not to mention the dead-cow Boris skull).' On 10 August, the Met Office issued a four-day amber warning for extreme heat. The alert was the longest they had ever put out and followed the first-ever red warning, which was announced in July when temperatures exceeded 40 degrees.

12 August 2022
Rob Murray
Telegraph

Author Salman Rushdie was left in a critical condition after being stabbed on stage in New York state. Rushdie had previously been in hiding for many years after the late Iranian leader Ayatollah Ruhollah Khomeini called for the author's death in retribution for his book, *The Satanic Verses* (1988), which many Muslims interpret as blasphemous. President Joe Biden praised Rushdie for his 'refusal to be intimidated or silenced'. According to the cartoonist, 'On such tragic occasions, images of mighty pens versus swords often come to mind. I've drawn too many of these. Here I wanted to comment on the creeping danger of self-censorship.'

15 August 2022
Peter Schrank
The Times

COOL......

ENERGY PRICE CAP FREEZE

Labour leader Keir Starmer called for the energy price cap to be frozen as part of his strategy to tackle the cost-of-living crisis. Starmer said that his plan, paid for by an expanded windfall tax on gas and oil giants, 'wouldn't let people pay a penny more' on their energy bills. The cap was due to rise in both October and January and experts predicted it could rise to £3,500 a year. Starmer's plans put pressure on the Conservative leadership candidates to increase their support for low-income households. A coalition of 70 charities signed an open letter to Liz Truss and Rishi Sunak warning that families on benefits faced a £1,600 shortfall unless the government provided more support.

16 August 2022
Brian Adcock
Guardian

Environmental campaign groups called for water companies to face prosecution after sewer discharges polluted coastlines. People were told it was unsafe to swim after human waste was pumped into the sea at beaches across eight counties from Cornwall to Northumberland. Water suppliers said the discharges were necessary to prevent flooding after rain from heavy thunderstorms landed on parched ground, but campaign organisations called for greater planning and punishment to prevent reoccurrences. Meanwhile, it was revealed that the annual bonuses paid to water company executives had increased by 20 per cent in 2021, even though most firms failed to meet their sewage pollution targets. In total, 22 water bosses paid themselves £24.8 million.

19 August 2022
David Simonds
Evening Standard

The former BBC journalist, Emily Maitlis, accused her past employer of being infiltrated by a Conservative Party agent who was seeking to 'pacify' the government. In 2020, Maitlis had been at the centre of a row after BBC chiefs decided she had breached impartiality rules during a *Newsnight* episode about Dominic Cummings who was chief advisor to the prime minister at that time. Maitlis implied that the corporation's swift and 'very public' apology following a Downing Street complaint had been initiated by an 'active agent of the Conservative party' who now acts as an 'arbiter of BBC impartiality'. She also speculated that the BBC was 'perhaps sending a message of reassurance directly to the government itself'.

26 August 2022
Dave Brown
Independent

On 26 August, it was announced that the energy regulator, Ofgem, had raised the energy price cap by more than 80 per cent to £3,549 per year. The revelation came as households were already budgeting for a tough winter, with soaring energy prices and rising inflation. Jonathan Brearley, the chief executive of Ofgem, said that the increase would have a 'massive impact' on households, and that 'it's clear the new prime minister will need to act further to tackle the impact of price rises'. While both Liz Truss and Rishi Sunak had promised support if they won the Conversative leadership contest, neither had given details of their policies – prompting critics to say that the candidates were burying their heads in the sand.

28 August 2022
Chris Riddell
Guardian

Liz Truss pulled out of her interview with the BBC's Nick Robinson, saying she could no longer spare the time for the one-on-one sit down. Robinson tweeted that he was 'disappointed and frustrated' by the cancellation. Rishi Sunak's team accused Truss of 'avoiding scrutiny', while the Labour Party claimed that Truss did not want to answer questions because she had no 'serious answers' to the challenges facing the country. The ballot of Conservative Party members was due to close on 2 September. Truss was widely considered to be the favourite to become the next prime minister.

31 August 2022
Peter Brookes
The Times

Mikhail Gorbachev, the last leader of the Soviet Union, died at the age of 91. As leader of the USSR from 1985 to 1991, Gorbachev was credited with introducing key political and economic reforms which helped to end the Cold War and take down the Iron Curtain. President Putin expressed his condolences, although he had previously criticised Gorbachev for policies that led to the fall of the Soviet Union – a collapse that Putin called the 'greatest geopolitical catastrophe of the century'. Meanwhile, on 24 August, Ukraine marked its Independence Day – the 31st anniversary of the country's vote in favour of breaking with the Soviet Union – exactly six months after Russia's invasion began.

31 August 2022
Christian Adams
Evening Standard